From Democracy To Democrazy

A Warning To All US Citizens

By Elizabeth Graham

ISBN: 978-8-9883978-1-6

Library of Congress control number 2021922551

This book is a revision of Democrazy, Version 2020

Testimonials

About The Book

Kirkus Professional Reviews. indie@kirkusreviews.com

Graham's comparative assessment between life in the U.S. and life in Russia is a deeply personal account of her own life. It is an intriguing and informative "must read" from a woman who is probably among the best-informed Americans on the terrifying realities concerning Putin's motivations, the KGB/FSB, business/crime in Russia, and most importantly the deep, dark clandestine relationship between Putin and Trump – a relationship which obstructed American politics from 2015 to today.

The book's real value lies in Graham's personal story, not only as an expert on Russian society, but as "a seventy-six-year-old White grandmother" and former Republican who finally came to terms with America's history of discrimination. Graham's astute commentary is also accompanied by an entertaining and informative assortment of political cartoons, graphs, and charts.

Kindle Customer

This book is a must-read for Americans who want to know true facts about what's happening to our country.. It takes courage to write about the truth and not fall into that "fake news" trap. This book will give you a stunning perspective. She also connects all the dots of the Trump administration and his partnership with Putin. Thank you, Elizabeth!

J. Sharpe

Elizabeth Graham brilliantly accounts her life's experiences with insight into the evil threat of Putin and more in a warning to us and the threat to our hard earned democracy.

"Shining a light on 2020"

Elizabeth Graham experienced Russia and Putin's power firsthand, thus she gained a even greater insight into the events of 2020 than most of us have gotten from cable news and newspapers. In her book, Democrazy 2020, she shows how Putin influenced our media and our election in his overall goal to destroy our precious democracy. Yes, it can happen here, and it nearly did. Read this book and see why we need to be aware of what is happening around us. I highly recommend it.

D. Jackowski

I was staying in a Marriot brand hotel near Chicago last year and while flipping through the cable channels I ran across RT. When checking it out I mentioned to the manager that I was surprised that RT was one of the cable choices. He didn't know what RT was so I told him, it's Russian Television. Elizabeth presents a excellent illustration of how subtle propaganda can influence behavior targeting emotional issues like race, trust in government and conspiracy. Social media provides a low cost conduit for inserting demagoguery and falsehoods into our political process. It's been shockingly effective. Thanks for your understanding of Russia's capabilities and motives.

N. Marshall

Elizabeth Graham tells us what we all should know already - that Putin, as the dictator of Russia, is out to weaken (destroy) the U.S.A., and that Trump essentially mimicked Putin in his efforts to destroy U.S. institutions and gain dictatorial power. She also calls out our fundamental historical flaw of racism, which we must acknowledge as we heal and improve our democracy. I would think she might be just another liberal, but she had many years experience working undercover with the USG and she also lived and worked in Russia, speaking Russian, and knowing the culture of Eastern Europe in a way most Americans just simply do not. Thanks for this eye-opening analysis and call to action to save our democracy from autocrats and wanna-be dictators.

An Amazon Customer

This book resonates with me as I am sure it will with others who read it. Glad to have a different perspective on Putin/Russia. So many parallels and warning signs with Russian politics and our own over the past few years. Glad this book focuses on those and ties them together. Worth the read!

k3oy

An eye opening educational book that defined the source, cause and effects of our recent former administration. Gives an unbiased perspective from someone who lived and worked among the Russians and Eastern Bloc European countries. A legitimate perspective our media failed to provide. Highly recommend.

Mark Walker

Ms. Graham brings a unique perspective on Putin, as well as Trump's relationships with Russians. She speaks Russian and some Ukrainian and worked for the CIA under-cover with a top-secret clearance. She lived in Russia for nearly 20 years. She also writes about why so many Americans were "brainwashed" in regard to Putin and Trump. Her explanations of how Russia operates to entrap foreigners - including Trump - and then threatens their loved ones is an eye-opener for most naive Americans. But then during the 2020 U.S. election we saw election workers lives threatened and Republican's opposed to Trump who were told their children would be butchered or murdered. The U.S. Republican Senate under Trump operated from fear of reappraisal exactly like the Russian DUMA - no one opposes Putin or they or a member of their family would die. This book is a timely true story every American should read and be aware of.

Unfortunately, there are too many Americans with closed minds. This book on Kindle was rated number one in three Amazon categories on July 12, 2023 - out of more than four million similar books in the market. A timely story every American should be aware of.

About The Author

Sister Mary Catherine DeSouza. BRAZIL
"Sister Mary Catherine said that the help her Brazilian community received from Elizabeth have helped them make it through the difficult times. Elizabeth came into my life and opened it up."

C. W. Knapp, Regional Director of the USAID Environmental Policy and Technology Office/Moscow. RUSSIA.
"Elizabeth, I think you are the right person to tackle this interesting and challenging consulting assignment with the Russian government."

Minister Merbolet Chakipov, the Kazakhstan International Business Committee. KAZAKHSTAN.
"Dear Elizabeth: It brings me great pleasure to be able to work with you. I think that you will bring to Kazakhstan many new ideas and business concepts."

Sergei Glasev, Deputy Minister for Foreign Economic Relations of the Russian Federation. Full member of the Russian Academy of Sciences, EEC Commission member of the board, and Minister in charge of Integration and Macroeconomics. Author of *Genocide:Russia and the New World Order*, RUSSIA.
Letter to Graham: "On behalf of the Russian Federation, I would like to personally welcome you to Moscow and offer my services should you require them over

the next few years. Your presence in Moscow will help establish an atmosphere of great cooperation between our two great nations."

Sergei Glasev's Letter to the Honorable Ambassador Robert Strauss, U.S. Embassy, Moscow, Russia (translated from Russian to English)
"It is my honor to express my highest respect to you. I would like to attract your attention to the development problems of business relations between Russian defense enterprises and American firms. The Ministry would like to work with Elizabeth Graham in creating a data base on defense enterprises. Please respectfully consider the possibility of rendering financial assistance to this project from the 'technical assistance funds' allocated by the U.S. Government. I look forward to our fruitful cooperation."

Ms. Amy Nolen Osborn, Program Officer for the Embassy of the United States of America and the U.S. Foreign Commercial Service. UKRAINE.
"As you are aware, Ukraine has had to depend on Russia for all relative and technical information needs over the past 75 years. It is our hope that your bi-cultural expertise will assist both Russia and Ukraine with the capacity to move Ukraine toward independence."

Timothy McCune, President 2MS Incorporated, RUSSIA & USA.
"This letter was written to certify and acknowledge that Elizabeth Graham is an Independent Consultant on Russian Affairs to 2MS, Inc. Her expertise related to Russian business has proved to be invaluable to our corporation and resulted in our firm acquiring a contract to assist in the Omsk International Airport construction project."

Josh Zander, A business and financial consultant to the Center for Citizen Initiatives (CCI) in St. Petersburg, RUSSIA.
"I have known and worked closely with Elizabeth since 1995. At that time she was the Acting President/Director of Russian Operations for CCI in Russia which

had six offices throughout the country. During this timeframe, she also worked in an advisory capacity to the City of St. Petersburg via the Leontiff Centre. She has been able to bring together what have often been disparate elements and interests, and bridge considerable cultural gaps and experiential differences to create functional, practical projects – usually with U.S. Government contracts – that accomplished the necessary objectives. Because these contracts were multi-million dollar awards, she also had to deal with local Russian "security" issues and threats to her life as well as Russian staff. She has made presentations – in English or in Russian – to Ambassador Morningstar (the U.S. special representative of President Clinton), Ambassador Pickering (the U.S. Ambassador to Russia), to John Evans (the U.S. Consul-General in St. Petersburg), to Mayor Anatoli Sobchak (former Mayor of St. Petersburg), to Mr. Alexander Yakovlev (Governor), and to other U.S. and Russian government officials."

Gerald A. Simon, Chairman of the Editorial Board for the Journal of Management Consulting (The Forum for Management Consultants Worldwide). RUSSIA.

"I had an opportunity to work with, as well as observe, Elizabeth (in St. Petersburg) in her role as manager under normal as well as crisis conditions. For calmness under fire, for creativity and flexibility, for just being a good person who doesn't play games with others, and for just being open and direct in her feelings with both locals (Russians) and we "foreigners" (Americans) – while still extremely savvy and sensitive to local facts on the ground – I give her very high marks."

Dr. Serguei M. Babenko, Associate Professor and Associate Chairman at Moscow Institute of Radiotechnology, Electronics and Automation. RUSSIA

"Ms. Graham is the brilliant specialist in cross-cultural issues and information technology. She is very famous in Russia. She was invited by the Russian government to the Russian-United States summit in Washington, D.C. She presented there several proposals which were submitted. She will represent nine international informational businesses (including Janes from the U.K.) in Moscow and will receive funding from the Russian government to coordinate Russian manufacturing standards with worldwide standards. Ms. Graham has a heart of gold and helps people all over the world."

The Honorable President of Rwanda, Paul Kagame. RWANDA
"Elizabeth, I have learnt of the great work the Craft Center does in empowering various artisans around the world, and I am convinced that these are positive efforts in the fight against poverty. May I take this opportunity to invite you to Rwanda to share your expertise with our local artisans."

The President of the United States, Mr. Joseph Biden. UNITED STATES
"Elizabeth, everywhere the First Lady and I go, we are constantly inspired by the grit and determination of the American people. Through trials and triumph, we will always be a Nation where hope runs deep and optimism reigns. Folks like you remind me of that truth every day. Keep the faith.

This book is dedicated to my father. As a child, he told me regularly that "I was no better than anyone else in this world . . . but I was also no worse."

It is dedicated to my three children and to my three grandchildren. May they all live their lives appreciative of the words handed down by my father, their grandfather and great-grandfather! Know that I love each of you dearly and more than words can express.

And to my oldest daughter, Lize, who died in Tokyo, Japan on July 11, 2016. She befriended everyone that she met, worked and traveled the world, and spoke eight languages. Her ashes are now among the Maasai Tribe in Kenya where she worked with children. Her spirit plagues my soul daily, along with that of her father who was my first husband. He died way too young of a brain tumor.

Special thanks to my editor Diane for her superb editing skills and precious time. Byron contributed his time to help with all the graphics and charts, and Don provided the SEO and website work that catapulted this book from ordinary to exceptional. John was my first Russian instructor and long-time friend.

Others who contributed – knowingly or unknowingly - to this book must be recognized and generously thanked.

Michael H.	Alexander D.	Karen P.	Heather T.
Zhana B.	Tim M.	Jeffrey T.	Lidiya V.
Walter F.	Penny & Jim	Ole B.	Bakhtiyar K.
John S.			

Dostoyevsky said: *"BEAUTY WILL SAVE THE WORLD,"* but ugly violence and hatred will DESTROY all if we allow it.

This book is about believing in right from wrong and why/how the United States was caught in an evil, repulsive, and dangerous vortex from 2016 to 2020 and beyond.

Elizabeth Graham, the author.

Keep in mind that this book was written partially from a Russian mind-set. My heart lives in the United States, but my soul lives in Russia. This point of view is far different than all other books on the market today about our democracy, our society, our country, and our former President – Mr. Trump.

Elizabeth Graham, the author.

THIS BOOK IS A WARNING TO ALL US CITIZENS.
IT CAN (AND IS) HAPPENING HERE.

Contents

LIST OF ILLUSTRATIONS AND DRAWINGS

Chapter 8

Preface

George Floyd was murdered in the summer of 2020. Like so many others across the U.S. and around the world, my gut response was disbelief, outrage, and even blind fury. The news replayed his death over and over and over. I reached a saturation point where I could no longer watch this man – this human - die on live TV. My heart grieved for his family. Still more, I mourned for our country. ANOTHER Black man[1] had been killed at the hands of our police. There is a malevolent tragedy playing out across our country, and now – finally – spectators are recording these murders. These recordings provide proof of this injustice and criminal immoralities.

To understand the context of this book, the reader needs to be acquainted with why my reaction to this evil was so grave as well as significant. I am not an African American. I am not politically radical – left or right. For many years, I voted as a registered Independent, but prior to that, I was a Republican because that was my father's party. My political affiliation changed when George Floyd died. I am not young, full of pervasive or activist energy running through my blood. I am a seventy-plus year-old White grandmother.

My appreciative and empathetic views of the United States have been fashioned by family – my father's philosophy on life is that you do not judge others by their looks, possessions, positions, jobs, or status, or money, but by how they treat other people. It is about one word, "respect." I worked undercover with a top secret clearance and inside our federal government for more years than I wish to mention or that I am allowed to discuss, and worked outside this country and within communist and dictatorship systems for decades. I value the diversity of our country perhaps more than most citizens, yet grasp the fear and trepidation that accompanies the "unknowns" of other cultures, races, languages, and especially those in positions of power.

I grew up in a Republican family where both parents worked undercover for the CIA, and they freely expressed their dislike of "Blacks" without providing any justification for these feelings. Those were the days of Martin Luther King Jr., John Robert Lewis, and Black Panthers; a period in U.S. history where Marches were televised on old-boxed Sylvania televisions. My father's face would be beet-red while watching the demonstrations in Selma and other cities. To him, demonstrations meant civil unrest and a lack of appreciation or respect of the democratic lifestyle he fought to preserve in World War II. He was a prisoner of war in Germany. I never understood his anger, and he and I would heatedly discuss racial inequality at the daily dinner table. My father would drink heavily only once a year. He never spoke about the war except on New Year's Eve when he would remember a dear friend and soldier who "took a bullet for him" in the war.

Martin Luther King Jr. taught nonviolence; a philosophy that paralleled Gandhi's and Jesus', and he was outspoken about the ineffectuality of violence. His ability to speak eloquently and to lead others in nonviolent but significant societal movements was unsurpassed. He would probably react to the recent violence with the same words as the Floyd family. They have asked demonstrators to denounce the looting and viciousness since this is not what George Floyd would have wanted.[2]

The last five to six decades have not brought the U.S. populace or government leaders closer to fulfilling the truth enshrined in the Declaration of Independence that all men are created equal. Despite our younger generation displaying far less race consciousness, our police have continued the venomous chant of bigotry. It cannot be ignored - from Baltimore to Los Angles and Cleveland to Phoenix – Blacks have been killed by local police, or if not killed, they have been unjustly and disproportionately beaten or imprisoned.

> **This lie of American equality has set a countrywide standard of dishonesty and deceitfulness for generations of Americans.**

I wish that I could say that these police officers are a "few bad apples" embedded in certain police departments or in certain parts of the country. But when this clearly identified pattern of bloodthirsty, inhumane, murderous reoccurrence extends to almost every major city in our nation, it cannot be disregarded – not by me or anyone in this country.

This book is factual and brief. It attempts to explain only the last few decades of racial profiling and killings, and it also discloses other serious issues in our democracy that every American needs to investigate and work toward solving. This includes the two-party political system and the appalling and megalomaniac behavior of our past president – Donald Trump, especially concerning his relationships with Russia.

So much has already been written about racism by educated authors, discussed in the halls of Congress, within state governments, and in every major city across the U.S. Racial disparity has been endlessly deliberated in national media, and especially in Black homes where parents feel the desperate need to protect their innocent children from this atrocity.

The Civil Rights Movement of the 1960s did not succeed or fail but was a meaningful ongoing chapter in U.S. history. Martin Luther King Jr. was the voice of justice for this battle. John Robert Lewis, who died of pancreatic cancer in July 2020, was a magnificent pillar of peaceful demonstrations to fight racial injustice despite suffering a broken skull, bloody beatings, and incarceration. At the age of twenty-five, he was one of the leaders of the Selma March[3] which began with a handful of organizers. The plan was to walk in twos across the Edmund Petrus Bridge, named after a former KKK President, and continue from Selma to Montgomery. State Troopers, many of them on horseback, met the crowd and beat them back. John Robert Lewis suffered a cracked skull and other injuries. When the marchers were released from the hospital, a new March was formed.[4]

Instead of a few hundred nonviolent protestors, there were over 25,000 angry but peaceful citizens walking together arm-in-arm <u>requesting equality</u> – in a country founded on "all men are created equal."[5]

Lewis went on to affectionately become the "conscience" of our Congress.[6] What is impossible to determine is if our current chapter in history is near the beginning or end of racism or whether American society will ever be able to eradicate this evil, irrational behavior? Is racism just a fear of the unknown and ignorance, is it inexcusable hatred, or is it brainwashing handed down from generation to generation? Is it a universal global human defect or a failed rationalization of slavery in the U.S.?

Racism in the United States exists. It's way past time to deal with it.

Racism asserts the supremacy of one race over another, but common sense should tell you that this is simply not true. You are no more or less "human" than President Kagame in Rwanda, a Black mother and children living on the south side of Chicago, or the Queen/King of England.

We cannot refute the physical differences because they are universal, but in my many years abroad, I witnessed that NO RACE is better or superior. This experience includes living and/or working in all of the former Soviet Republics (15 countries including Central Asia), Bosnia, Africa (5 nations including Rwanda), India, Pakistan, Afghanistan, the Far East (4 nations), and South America (3 nations). In Russia alone, there are identified 190 ethnic groups[7] with just as many languages spoken and cultures embraced. Eighty percent of the population is Russian, and during the Soviet period, every child was educated in the Russian language and most learned English.

My more than twenty years in the Soviet Union, Russia, and then Central Asia allowed me to become bi-cultural and multi-lingual, but more importantly, it allowed me to observe my own country from abroad. Just like colleges and universities in the U.S. have courses called Soviet Studies and often refer to Russia as the "evil empire", Russia has courses focused on the United States and especially concerning our violent racial history. While I never attended these courses, I did meet a professor who wrote about U.S. history. He shared with me some of his course material. To view my own country through the eyes of a rival nation allowed me to sort through the propaganda and combine this information with my own experiences. The application of this process was uncomfortable yet it provided a *unique and distinctive perspective* on American life - especially concerning prejudges and racism - and forced me to examine my own soul and my own birthplace.

As a child, I was taught that the United States of America was a nation of heroes, of human kindness, of honesty, of equal opportunity for all, of justice, and literally the best country in the world. In looking back at that childhood, I now wonder if these thoughts were an idealist and perhaps childish viewpoint – or my father's indoctrination so I would grow up to join the CIA like him. I still deeply believe in and love our form of democracy and freedom, but as an adult and after spending most of my career abroad – I witnessed many other countries, races, conflicts and how other cultures and governments operate – some good and some not so good.

In 1994, the full horror of racism in Rwanda violently killed about 800,000 people in three short months.[8] This chilling tribal war pitted Tutsis against Hutus. Horrific images filled our TV screens and the scale and violence of this genocide were impossible to grasp. At the personal invitation of President Paul Kagame's government[9], I traveled to Kigali in 2002 for a consulting job. The lessons shared were not just about nonprofit management, income-generation concepts, micro-credit programs, disease control, small craft business development, gender-based violence, or orphan care – most of my past employment nonprofit experiences. For me, these were personal lessons about the extremes of hatred and humanitarian crisis – and racial strife. This war was neighbor against neighbor and human carnage and slaughter. As I danced with a large group of laughing young orphans in a sizable community thatched-roof hut on a dirt floor,

I was sobbing. I wanted to share their joy while dancing to the rhythm of their ankle bells, their songs, and their other handmade musical instruments. Instead, all I could see were those children's noticeable scars of war – some were missing a hand, an arm, an ear, a foot, an eye; others bore signs of brutality such as machete scars on their backs, stomachs, or even heads. My visceral reaction to those children's injuries was an onslaught of throbbing and consuming grief – a learning experience that will never be forgotten.

The following year in 1995, the city of Srebrenica in Bosnia became the site of Europe's worst massacre since World War II.[10] The Serbian (Christian) army staged a brutal takeover of this small, intimate mountainous town and its surrounding region. Over a period of only five days, the Serbian soldiers separated the Bosnian (Muslim) families and systematically murdered over 7,000 men and boys in fields, schools, and warehouses.[11] Overall, this ethnic cleansing war began in 1992 and lasted until 1995, with an estimated 250,000 killed and over 50,000 women raped – more rapes than any other recorded war.[12]

United Nations troops intervened to stop the slaughter. When this *religious and ethnic war* ended, the Muslim women of Srebrenica helped investigators find mass graves, identify victims, and fundraise for a memorial. In 2003, USAID and World Learning invited me to visit Bosnia. The purpose of this consultancy was to analyze the current living conditions of Bosnia-Herzegovina in terms of socio-economic sectors, potential income generation ideas, public policies and laws, and the commonality and education levels of the Muslim women involved. My task was to formulate recommendations to USAID and to U.S. Ambassador Bond for potential income-generation opportunities for the Muslim women who wished to return to their pre-war homes, which they still legally owned. Many of their homes were now occupied by Christians. This consulting task was labeled "mission impossible" by many individuals who were willing to openly discuss the full impact and implications of this assignment. Each and every potential income generation idea faced a myriad of obstacles – all fueled by hundreds of years of racial and ethnic hatred. Muslim women could not pick mushrooms in the hills because there still were land mines, or they might be raped. They could not open a pasta factory because the majority Serbs would not buy their products. They could not open a dairy and sell eggs, milk, yogurt, and cheese. The reason was that the Serbian-controlled utility company would turn off the electricity to the Muslim business while leaving the electricity turned on in a Serbian business next door. This consultancy resulted in recommending these women organize a nonprofit craft business of hand-knitted sweaters and other handmade products, which are now successfully sold globally in major department stores such as Harrods in London, Bloomingdales in New York, and Neiman Marcus in Dallas – when shopping just look for the label that says "Handmade in Bosnia."

One Muslim woman told me that the week before I came to Srebrenica, she passed the man on the street who killed her three sons and her husband while she was forced to watch. After he killed her family, he raped her while other Serbian men stood by and laughed. When she walked past him on the street, he spat on her. In interviewing many of these Muslim women, my emotions were again raw and agonizing. I was constantly fighting back tears and my chest felt oppressive heaviness as I listened to their individual gruesome experiences. July 11, 2020, was the twenty-five-year anniversary of this immoral bloodbath. Today the Muslim women of Srebrenica are still recovering the bones of their loved ones through DNA testing. Their immeasurable sorrow is never-ending.

And in the U.S., a century has passed since the Tulsa, Oklahoma massacre and it's been about sixty years since the Bloody Sunday March in Selma, Alabama. Blood-shed in the U.S. due to racial hatred is ongoing and as of 2023 shows no sign of vanishing.

Fostering democracy around the World has been a foundation of U.S. foreign policy for many decades. But the ugly face of U.S. racism and violence has diminished the world's view of our country as a shining example of democracy – of what we call the "free world." Let's face it; we are no longer the global leader that we were only a few short years ago. Any U.S. resident must recognize this and then grasp the new character of living in our badly flawed form of democratic government. This book attempts to explain and warn all Americans about the events in our country from 2015 to 2020 and beyond.

Our system is failing on so many fronts, and the ongoing racial hatred, mass murders, and police brutality are just a few of the obvious and agonizing illustrations of our failure. The death of George Floyd, an innocent U.S. citizen, is an example of how U.S. police-instigated violence resulted in protest demonstrations in every major city across America and around the world. Yes, the whole world was watching, judging, evaluating, and then:

Tens of thousands of people around the world protested police action in the United States.

The message delivered was loud and clear that people in other countries do not agree with the U.S. form of democracy whereby people of color are violently murdered by our police – and they are right! These other countries are telling U.S. citizens that "we do not want a democracy like yours." Yet, the U.S. Government continues to push our form of democracy on other societies. This must stop.

First, the billions of U.S. dollars sent abroad more often than not goes astray and not where it is intended. I know this happens because I was the senior manager of several large NGOs abroad receiving multi-million dollar U.S. Government grant awards. The proposals for these grants are usually written in the U.S. in response to government "requests for proposals" (RFPs) and which adhere to U.S. laws. The trick is to comply with U.S. regulations and U.S. contract requirements while understanding and meeting the local operational needs and local laws. For instance, the West would call some expenses a "bribe" while in many other countries it is considered a normal operating expense or cost of doing business – but a legal "receipt" is required for all U.S. and international government audits. Second, the majority of the world does not want to duplicate our democracy – they only want our money. Third, our own country needs these dollars to balance our enormously negative federal budget.

An example of how the U.S. has wasted millions of dollars abroad include the Central Asian American Enterprise Fund (CAAEF) which was a U.S. Congressional mandate of $150,000,000 - seed money created by the U.S. Government as an investment to foster start-up companies in Central Asia after the collapse of communism.[13] I was a consultant to CAAEF on a pharmaceutical joint venture in Uzbekistan. CAAEF was managed by USAID (the United States Agency of International Development) and a Board of Directors which appeared to be vastly inexperienced concerning the business environment of Central Asia.

There were multiple million dollar deals that were fraudulent and that lost money through deceptive overhead. They even purchased businesses that did not exist – resulting in a loss of $80 million dollars.[14] As a consultant, I was asked to review the JV (Joint Venture) contracts in both English and Russian. These contracts were drawn-up by New York attorneys who were vastly illiterate about how local Central Asian government and companies operate. After reviewing the English versions of the JV documents, I found that they did not read the same in Russian. The Russian attorneys, working with the Uzbek JV partner, would normally include "tricky" wording. In the case of this pharmaceutical project – "if the agreed-to collateral was not fully contributed by both partners within a certain timeframe, the JV was null and void." The local partner allowed CAAEF to pay millions of dollars for startup expenses and then at some point they would point out this clause in the contract and sever the JV agreement. The Uzbeks never intended to contribute their collateral as promised in the English-language version of the agreement. The naivety of the Americans – both businessmen and attorneys was disconcerting. The Uzbek JV partner walked away with a fully equipped new business and a full warehouse of product – the Americans lost millions of tax-payer money. "Many experts believed that the fund's failures lie mainly in the Board's lack of knowledge about about the local business environ ment."[15]

Another example of American naivety was the election of Donald Trump. He had been courted and manipulated by the Russians for many years – thinking he was "doing business with Russians" but instead they used Trump to funnel millions of dollars of black cash into the U.S. via his real estate deals.[16] Americans who voted for Trump because he was a Republican, also believed he was a good business man. This man had declared bankruptcy four times and no bank in the U.S. would loan him more money.[17] This is not an indication of business knowledge, but perhaps of a person who commits fraud for self-serving reasons – line his own pockets. The Russians were anxious to work with Trump and loan him money – only Trump was too naïve to understand the Russian motivations.

Additionally, every syndicated TV news outlet, nationally distributed news-papers across the U.S. and others described Trump as self-obsessed, narcissistic, vulgar, a racist, and degrading to women.

Why else would he singularly target to eliminate progressive accomplishments made by President Obama or deny that Obama was even born in the U.S.? Why else would he work to eliminate most forms of immigration to our country – a nation 100% founded by immigrants – which includes two of his three wives? His constant conspiracy theories about how the election was stolen from him is a lie. In fact after the **2016 election**, Trump "claimed massive voter fraud – without any evidence."[18] This time he said Clinton stole the popular vote from him.

His attempts to pervert the election results by pressuring Jeffrey Clark, who was then the Acting Head of the Justice's Department Civil Division, to persuade other top leaders to alter and publicly denounce the election results deviated from our democratic form of government.[19] He pressured Republican Governors to do a vote recount, only to learn what the rest of the country already knew – Biden won the election. The cost of this recount in Arizona alone was approximately $6 million dollars[20] – wasted money that could have gone to reduce our federal deficit or for border issues in Arizona. The U.S. electoral voting system is NOT CORRUPT. You need to live in a communist or dictatorship country to truly understand corrupt elections.

Trump's behavior is like the dictators whom he openly admires – Vladimir Putin and Kim Jong-un. I recognized Trump's dictatorship-like behavior because I lived in Russia when Putin assumed power. During Putin's first few years, numerous reporters and media workers, those opposed to him because of his KGB background, were either murdered in cold blood,[21] disappeared, or changed careers.

The Washington Post reporter Robyn Dixon wrote and published an article on September 24, 2002.[22] She states: "After authorities threatened to prosecute staff at Novaya Gazeta, Russia's only remaining independent newspaper, its political editor decided he had no choice but to suspend operations. Kirill Martynov sought refuge in Latvia, along with 53 of the paper's staff, intent on starting a new European version despite having no money to finance it."[23]

The New York Times printed an article written by Celestine Bohlen in May 12, 2000 titled "Putin Defends Police Raid on Media Company."[24] In this article she says: "Mr. Putin, now five days in office as Russia's second president, has moved briskly this week to strengthen Moscow's control over the country's unruly provinces (and cities)" – and control of all sources of media."[25] Three months after Putin's inauguration, "it was estimated that 21 journalists have been killed since Putin came to power" in Russia in contract-style murders.[26] The Committee to Protect Journalists (CPJ) wrote in July 2000[27] "Igor Domnikov, from Novaya Gazeta was a reporter and editor for the twice-weekly Moscow paper, died two months after being struck in the head with a heavy object in the entryway of his apartment building in May 12th, 2000. Sergey Novikov, Radio Vesna owner who was 36 years old and owner of the independent radio station that often criticized the provincial government, was shot four times in the stairwell of his apartment building. Three days before the killing, Novikov participated in a television panel on alleged corruption in the deputy governor's office. Sergey Ivanov (30 years old), Lada-TV was shot five times in the head and chest in front of his apartment building. Lada-TV was a significant force on the local political scene."[28] This sadistic list of reporters killed goes on and on.

I lived in KV 44 (apartment 44 on the top floor), Oruzheniya Pereulok ½, 1-Podyed in Moscow 125009. One afternoon I heard gun shots and looked out my balcony window. On the street below was a woman lying in a pool of blood which was striking against the dirty Moscow city snow. Two days later, an elderly neighbor told me that the dead woman was a reporter and had been executed for her criticism of President Putin. She said this in such a nonchalant voice, that I had to ask her to repeat it. She shrugged her shoulders and dispassionately said "such is life and death in Russia under KGB rule." I never learned the reporter's name and there was no mention of her death in local newspapers or on Russian TV.

The West, and especially Americans, are incredibly naïve about Putin and Russia. Simply put, he is ruthless, still a trained KGB (which became the FSB in 1995)[29] officer at heart, and will stop at nothing to destroy his arch enemy - the United States, whom he blames for the breakup of the Soviet Union. Putin is a man who often speaks about world domination and first on his list is the United States and second is France.[30]

The Putin-Trump similarities are evident and recognizable. Most Americans just do not sit up and pay attention – and these similarities are almost beyond fathoming for most Americans. There are election workers across the U.S. who have received death threats.[31] The reason for these threats is that they refused to change the votes so they favored Trump. There are Republicans who did not support Trump and voted to impeach him whose families have been intimidated and frightened - including death threats on children.[32] How can anyone in the United States think this is how a normal democratic government operates?

In fact, Trump's undemocratic behavior was clearly visible for the whole world to see at the Helsinki Summit with President Putin on July 16, 2018.[33] After their private meeting, they walked together toward the podiums to speak with the press. Putin walked strong and confident, while Trump appeared to have seen a ghost. He looked pale, his shoulders were hunched over and his head was down. He looked like a child who had just seen damming evidence of a wrong-doing. Putin, on the other hand, was beaming and happy.

"As they approach the podium, Putin is the confident one, while Trump has none of his usual bluster. Bending forward is the classic posture of submission; here Trump hints at a possible psychological dynamic between them."[34]

While standing next to Putin, Trump commented that he "believed Putin's denial of election interference over the findings of U.S. intelligence."[35] The CIA Director, John Brennan, called it "nothing short of treasonous" and John Mc-

Cain described it as "one of the most disgraceful performances by an American president in memory." [36]

During that private meeting without American translators or reporters, Putin potentially showed Trump porno photos of himself with Russian prostitutes or Putin explained to Trump the ruthless and lethal repayment terms of doing business with or borrowing money from Russian Oligarchs or others. Trump just quietly agreed with Putin on all issues and denounced U.S. intelligence. ASK YOURSELF WHY?

"HELSINKI SUMMIT", ARTIST MIKE KEEFE, COURTESY OF CAGLE CARTOONS

US intelligence is perhaps the best in the world. I know this from an inside observation seat.

In *Russian Roulette*, a book written by Michael Isikoff and David Corn, they state the following:

"*It was the afternoon of January 6, 2017, and for two hours the president-elect had sat in a conference room at Trump Tower and listened to the leaders of the U.S.*

intelligence community brief him on an extraordinary document: a report their agencies had produced concluding that the Russian government had mounted a massive covert influence campaign aimed at disrupting the country's political system and electing him president of the United States.

When the spy chiefs – Director of National Intelligence James Clapper, CIA Director John Brennan, and National Security Agency Director Admiral Michael Rogers – left the room, one of them stayed behind. FBI Director James Comey then handed Trump . . . a two-page synopsis of reports prepared by a former British spy alleging that Trump and his campaign had actively collaborated with Moscow. The memo claimed that Russian intelligence had collected compromising material on Trump that could be used to blackmail him, including a tape of him engaging in sordid behavior with prostitutes in a Moscow hotel room." [37]

The information from British Intelligence had not been confirmed by the FBI as of the beginning of 2017. Eventually both men assigned to confirm this British intelligence were fired by Trump. Issikoff and Corn go on to say:

"However, the U.K. and the U.S. intelligence communities were giving Trump a "heads-up". For national security reasons, these men were warning Trump that his relationship with Russia had to change. It didn't change, but became more covert and undemocratic..." [38]

"Soviets use time-honored 'honey-trap' techniques to snare foreigners.[39] As far back as history has been written, sex has been used to entrap men. The Soviets and then the Russians used sexual blackmail – called "kompromat (compromise) on any foreigner possible."[40] Every single hotel room across Russia where a foreigner stays has cameras and listening devices in the walls and the ceiling. An Indian diplomat, code named PROKHOR, in the India Embassy in Moscow was recruited this way.[41]

In the case of Trump, his characteristics were ideally suited for the KGB/FSB kompromat. He was operating large businesses in the U.S. and elsewhere and these businesses were failing. They could easily be used to laundry Russian dirty money – multi-million dollars (called black cash). He previously had connections with U.S. prostitutes and ended up in court battles over potential bribe monies paid to them. The New York bribery case has not closed as of 2023.[42] He was closely connected with Ghislaine Maxwell and Jeffrey Epstein who both were convicted of running an underage call service for wealthy clients.[43]

Trump's massive ignorance about Russian business practices was apparent. Also, he had declared bankruptcy four times, which demonstrated to the Russians that he not repay his debtors – an ideal target for Russian kompromat. Trump has an enormous ego and loved the lavish attention he was receiving from Russians. Americans think this is normal graciousness, but it is how Russians entice their victims – they first befriend them and then trap them. It made Trump feel like an influential and important person. He wanted a Trump Tower in Moscow and he was lured by this promise. Last, Trump's businesses were in deep financial trouble. His taxes[44] have revealed massive (multi-million dollar) financial losses, so he was in need of operational cash. The U.S. banks refused to loan him money due to his constant business losses and his four bankruptcies. Trump suddenly found mega-million dollar cash transactions via Russian-funded real estate deals in the U.S.[45] This all led to Trump being indebted to Putin – a masterful spy who knows how to manipulate his subjects to get what he wants – and this could have included Top Secret nuclear capabilities of the US and other countries, or other military Secret information. Trump took hundreds of Top Secret and Secret documents from the White House, apparently which cannot be found. It is my assumption that these documents did not "just disappear," and they may even be in adversarial hands.

Trump and Putin had a minimum of sixteen private conversations since Trump became President of the United States.[46] What was said is unknown. As a result, Donald Trump has consistently set a precedent and an obvious ongoing pattern of opposition toward NATO and this animosity extended too many U.S. European allies. One of Russia's foremost strategic objectives has been to eliminate the NATO Alliance, which was created shortly after the end of World War II to ensure a balance of world power.[47] Second on Russia's strategic list is the withdrawal of U.S. troops from all or many European locations, but especially Germany.[48] For Trump to reduce the number of U.S. troops in Germany and other locations was an undeniable coup for Putin and a clear warning to every U.S. citizen and our European friends. It disclosed that Trump's decisions and actions were possibly under the control of Russian leadership. Russia, as the largest of the former Soviet Bloc countries, still operates with old-world communist and KGB principles. Those who believe that communism in Russia is gone are sadly mistaken – however under Putin, the country has transitioned from old-world communism - a sociopolitical, philosophical, and economic ideology - to a dictatorship.

I have lived in several communist and dictatorship countries. In Kazakhstan, I experienced life in a dictatorship where the leader truly cares about the country, yet still exhibits dictator behavior. President Nursultan Nazarbayev[49] – who served as the President of Kazakhstan from 1990 to 2019 (as a member of the Communist Party) developed their natural resources, including gas and oil, and used those funds to build Astana, which is the new capital of the country. It is a magnificent city that rivals the capitals of European countries.

I lived in Almaty which was the former capital of Kazakhstan. My large apartment overlooked a well-groomed park and I walked my dogs there daily. One weekend a month I would have an "American-style" home-made breakfast buffet with eggs benedict and banana and lemon cream pies made from recipes from my page-torn *Joy of Cooking*. The five U.S. Ambassador's for Central Asia were also stationed in Almaty along with a large U.S. Embassy staff. Many of them attended my monthly buffet along with Americans stationed in Pakistan and Afghanistan.

In Turkmenistan, I barely escaped the country before being imprisoned for "holding Christian religious meetings" in a Muslim country. I was living there operating a micro-credit program which I designed. It was funded by USAID (United States Agency for International Development) ($800,000 for operating costs) and CAAEF (Central Asia American Enterprise Fund) contributed $2 million for micro-credit loans. One morning I left my rental home to face a Turkmen Government black Zil (a large Russian-manufactured automobile often used by government officials) in my driveway. Two men presented me with official documents written in Turkmen, which I could not read, and they asked me in Russian to sign them. I refused and told them I needed to speak with my Turkmen translator. Later that day I learned that the documents were an admission of my "guilt" and said that I had placed meeting notices to discuss Christianity on telephone poles around the city of Ashgabat. I did not post notices, nor have religious meetings, nor did I bring a Bible to Turkmenistan. I informed USAID and left the country within days. Because they wanted me to depart, I was allowed to take the antiques, rugs, and works of art[50] I had collected without local Customs confiscating them. I was lucky – and could have just been killed or imprisoned, but then those American organizations contributing millions of dollars for this program would have pulled their support and money out of Turkmenistan.

Afghanistan shares a northern border with Turkmenistan, as well as Tajikistan and Uzbekistan. About the time I was in Turkmenistan, two American women in Afghanistan – Dayna Curry and Heather Mercer[51] - were imprisoned "for sharing a film about Jesus with a local family."[52] I am certain this is where the Turkmen government officials discovered the idea to threaten me with imprisonment. The Turkmen government wanted the American money, but did not want American management or oversight.

Micro-credit is a program symbolic of free markets. People could open a kiosk or store, sell goods, and make money outside their "government-assigned" employment which was typical in communist or dictatorship countries. When individuals are able to generate their own income, they have more control of their lives. Turkmenistan's dictator, Turkmenbashi[53] was fanatical about societal supremacy and command.

Tajikistan was the least developed country in Central Asia, and in the late 1990s if your passport said you were an American, you needed an armed escort to travel from the airport to your destination or to even move within the Capitol. In 1998, I was in Dushanbe, the country's Capitol, and was walking from the U.S. Embassy to an office nearby. The city was divided right down the middle by the two major combatant factions. Every person on the street had a rifle over their shoulder. I remember silently praying that no one would trip and start another civil war while I was there.

As the Central Asian Regional Director for Mercy Corps International (MCI), my job included oversight of programs in Kazakhstan, Turkmenistan, Kyrgyzstan, Uzbekistan, and Tajikistan with support to programs in Pakistan. MCI had formed a partnership with a small women's non-profit in Northern Tajikistan. One of the women in this group was missing a hand. When I asked what happened, she told me that her husband cut off her hand because his dinner was not ready when he wanted it. This incident alone justified building a women's rights program in Tajikistan, but also is an example of how dangerous this work could be.

While leaving Tajikistan to return to Kazakhstan, my armed escort delivered me directly to the airplane so the plane steps were only three or four feet from my car door. I was the only woman on the plane and the only person without a visible weapon. I was carrying a weapon, but it was concealed. The terrorism of 9/11 shook the entire world and changed travel laws globally, but up until 2002, anyone could carry a gun on a plane in the entire former Soviet territory – a landmass three times larger than the United States with eleven time zones.

The hostile behavior of Trump-ordered federal troops in Portland, Oregon, in July 2020[54] was a chilling reminder of my days living and working in communist or dictatorship countries.[55] Rather than deny this unconstitutional behavior, Trump tweeted that he planned to send federal troops to other cities managed by elected "Democratic or Black leadership," which he senselessly perceived as his opposition.[56] He specifically named Chicago, who had a Black female Mayor, as his next target for federal troop "invasion." The Taliban militant leadership in Afghanistan does the exact equivalent – a hostile take-over city by city.[57]

Putin regularly meets with regional political leaders and mayors of large cities. In such meetings, he continuously verifies their loyalty and submission. If he senses – even slightly – they are not 100% faithful and dedicated to his leadership – then they are quickly replaced, usually eliminated by murder and swapped with someone he prefers.

Initially, Trump's federal troops in Portland were unidentified, were using tear gas, and were forcibly escorting demonstrators into unmarked cars. This is NOT how a democracy operates. Step-by-step, Trump attempted to move OUR COUNTRY away from our democratic principles and toward a country controlled by one man, an autocratic, dictatorship form of government. With his total control of the Republican Senate, he nearly accomplished this task. This is exactly what Putin wished for.

Donald Trump has a sizable following of similar-thinking voters throughout the U.S. They ignore his vulgarity, his lack of leadership ability, his daily lies and constant conspiracy theories, his massive ignorance, his manipulation of the law for personal gain, his lack of even basic reading skills and retention, his racial slurs, and his four bankruptcies. They do not understand that he is mimicking Putin – because they reason Putin is 5,000 to 7,000 miles away from their homes. WRONG ASSUMPTION. In fact, he may not be mimicking Putin, but following directions from him.

These voters empathize with Trump. This list of "followers" includes elected members of the U.S. Senate, where almost no Republican voted to impeach him despite the fact that he was impeached twice in the House and the evidence (both times) was verifiable, indisputable, and one hundred percent accurate. These Republicans are just as afraid of Trump as the members of the Duma in Moscow are of Putin. These U.S. Senators just do not admit to their fear or perhaps do not recognize it.[58]

> **It's called a dictatorship - not a democracy - when the leader rules by instilling fear in elected government officials so they do as he wishes.**

Trump's followers provided verification, whether we understand this or not, that Trump as our President, was an example of our deteriorating democracy. They do not appear to grasp that they are allowing our country to move away from the basic freedoms that our founders envisioned, and they have demoralized and degraded our form of government.

> **They are not saving our democracy but destroying it.**

The reason that I understand this monumental shift is because I have witnessed and experienced life under Putin and lived in countries ruled by dictators. If you do a side-by-side comparison of Putin to Trump, their governing philosophies are almost identical. This alone is frightening. The only difference is that Putin is enormously more intelligent, knowledgeable, conniving, and actually has the tremendous all-encompassing power that Trump lacked – but was well on his way to achieving due to his specific version of victimization and intimidation. Trump is a bully – not by just shoving people around like most bullying boys in school - but by destroying lives.

The horrific spread of Covid-19 throughout the U.S. with its frightening death statistics demonstrated and substantiated Trump's lack of leadership ability and the extent of his dishonesty. The U.S. has consistently been the world's frontrunner in the total sum of virus cases, including the fastest-growing number of daily confirmed cases and the largest number of deaths.

The first case of this virus in the U.S. was diagnosed in January 2020.[59] Trump was forewarned about the potential spread and danger of this disease.[60] He took little to no action to protect U.S. citizens; in fact, he did the opposite. He did not recommend using a mask or 6-foot distancing. What he mentioned first was the use of Hydrochloroquine, a drug that has no ability to fight this disease. Second, he recommended a drug called Ivermectin created to deworm horses, but it poisons humans.[61] In Alabama and other primarily Republican states, hospital beds were filled with people who used these drugs because they listened to Trump.

"Covid and Horse Dewormer Claims," Artist – Dave Granlun, Courtesy of Cagle Cartoons

The spread of the coronavirus has been discernable. About half our country still had not received the free vaccines as of August 2021 amidst the resurgence of the Delta and the Omicron versions of COVID-19. Facts do not lie. The new, more deadly variants of the virus are primarily spreading in the Republican Southern states or middle-America, where people still are following Trump right into their graves.[62] In a TV interview[63], one Alabama woman said that she had not gotten the vaccine because she did not know what was in it. I would like to ask that same woman if she reads the ingredients for everything she consumes. I would trust American scientists and doctors more than I would trust the people in the "unknown origin" (probably China) that manufactures her breakfast cereals. This insanity of not getting vaccinated is killing innocent people and spreading this deadly disease.

It was not until July 2020 that Trump wore a mask in public.[64] So, while he would not cover his face to set an example for the rest of the nation, more than 145,000 Americans died.[65] By the end of 2020, the virus claimed the lives of over 400,000 Americans, and by mid-2021, over 600,000 Americans died of this disease, with an additional 250,000 more deaths expected by the end of the year.[66] By midway through 2022, over one million Americans died.[67] It is conceivable that half of their deaths could have been avoided if they had been encouraged by our former President to use the protection of a mask consistently. Masks have shown to be an effective deterrent to catching this highly contagious disease, and wearing a mask is far simpler, less expensive, and stress-free than a tube down your throat or a ventilator controlling your every breath – until a physician decides you can no longer breathe on your own and they turn off the ventilator. You then die.

Face masks became a political minefield instead of a key defense against the spread of COVID-19. Personal freedoms should not outweigh the good of society.

All societies have laws to protect their citizens.

Murderers go to prison for the rest of their lives for their brutal crimes. Individuals who have HIV/AIDS are convicted of a crime if they knowingly spread that virus. Southern Republican Governor's like Florida's DeSantis even threatened school official's salaries if schools required teachers and students to wear masks.[68] Thankfully, a Judge intervened and overruled the DeSantis statewide policy and allowed schools to decide.[69]

This policy in Florida is not only incredibly ill-informed but amounts to the punishment of education officials attempting to stop the spread of a deadly disease within their schools. This politicizing face masks shows a definite lack of caring and consideration for others and a lack of understanding about how a society should function to protect its citizens, which may be the same unenlightened mentality that demonstrates how our society also deals with racism.

For the 2024 election Republicans in our country are trying to decide between Trump and DeSantis as the next potential candidate for the U.S. Presidency. This is strong evidence that the Republican Party is in serious trouble.

With almost no meaningful COVID-19 leadership from the Trump Presidency – or the DeSantis Governorship of Florida - our economy and our citizens gravely suffered. Many businesses and factories have shut down; millions upon millions have filed for unemployment benefits, and the death rate continues to climb. Daily, Americans have suffered and died because Trump openly disagrees with medical experts.[70] Trump disparaged doctors who have studied infectious contagions for many years, while he has NO EDUCATION in this field. Those dying are loved mothers, fathers, children, and grandparents. Our country has surpassed all other nations in positive coronavirus cases. Wake up America, we are dying, and this virus is still spreading because our past President refused to listen to medical experts. Now some Republican Governors are doing the same thing! This inanity and absurdity are beyond description.

The United States has the most informed and educated medical experts and scientists in the entire world. Yet Trump, as well as several Republican Governors, choose to ignore their scholarly advice.[71] By disregarding, discounting, and snubbing the brilliant medical and science experts, Trump and Republican Governors who agree with him are potentially sentencing people to death. Why people would listen to a politician concerning health issues rather than an educated physician is beyond rationalization. You would not ask a politician to do heart surgery or fix a broken leg.

Covid is a lethal and highly contagious disease.

"Medical Tyranny", Artist – Randall Enos, Courtesy of Cagle Cartoons.

This book ties together the American form of racism with bigotry, biases, and hatred and connects it to our government and our police and our military – vital components of the U.S. Government. It explains how other countries view the U.S. due to our racism and our violence, our money-hungry attitudes, and explains why the United States is no longer the "leader of the free world."[72]

It demonstrates the puzzle pieces that were in play during Trump's four years as a President, and then concludes how so many intelligent Americans were unknowingly brain-washed to believe Trump's outrageous, dishonest and repetitive rhetoric – the same form of brainwashing used in Germany by Hitler to transform a peaceful society into blood-thirsty murderers filled with antisemitism and hatred. The January 6th Capitol riot is proof that Trump's brain-washing techniques were effective and dangerous.

It explains to Americans that Putin and his "gang" of KGB thugs are diligently working to destroy the United States from within. In order to do this, he uses the tools of: racism, violence, antisemitism, insurrection, cyberattacks, inflation, brainwashing, and isolationism. Most Americans do not associate these things with Putin and his ongoing internal destruction of the U.S.

He also has penetrated our system of government through blackmail, bribery, and money – perhaps billions of dollars. As a capitalist country – money can buy anything – including top-level government officials. I estimate that for every U.S. official or government worker caught working with the Russians, there will be ten more that are not caught.

Perhaps more importantly, this book explains the ties between the U.S. and Russia and between Trump and Putin – from someone who was born American, became bi-cultural (American to Russian), and who has lived and worked in both countries.

PREFACE – END NOTES

1 https:www.washingtonpost.com. "Police Shootings Data Base 2015 – 2023." "1,110 people have been shot and killed by police in the past twelve months." Written by Bill DeWayne Couch, 25 January 2023.

2 "George Floyd's brother implores protestors to stop looting," CBS News, June 2, 2020.

3 www.archives.gov/exhibits/eyewitness, "John Lewis – March from Selma to Montgomery."

4 Ibid.

5 Ibid.

6 https://wwwgasettenet.com. "John Lewis hailed as the 'conscience' of Congress. House Speaker Nancy Pelosi called Lewis the 'conscience of the Congress' who was 'revered and beloved on both sides of the aisle',..." Written by Bill Barrow and Andew Taylor, July 27, 2020.

7 https://en.wikipedia.org_wiki_List_of_ethnic-groups. "The Russian Federation is a multinational state with over 190 ethnic groups designated as nationalities, population of these groups varying enormously..."

8 www.history.com/topics/africa/rwandan-genocide. Facts, Response & Trials.

9 See his invitation letter in the Testimonial Section of this book.

10 https://en.wikipedia.org/wiki/Bosnian_War.

11 Ibid.

12 Ibid.

13 The New York Times, September 4, 2001, by B. Brauer, "U.S. Missteps Wasted Investments in Central Asian Economics, Critics Say."

14 Ibid.

15 Ibid.

16 https:www.americanprogress.org/article. "Following the Money: Trump and Russia-Linked Transactions ... At the heart of the inquiry into the alleged collusion between Trump and Russia is money. It provides concrete evidence of relationships, methods, and motives." Director, Media Relations, Sam Hananel. December 17, 2018.

17 Quora, "Why haven't the US banks been willing to lend Trump money for years? John Sumak, Retired Electro-Mechanical Engineering said "I doubt Trump could get a car loan at one of those buy-here/pay-here everyone gets approved car lots." Trump defaulted and declared bankruptcy four times.

18 https//www.usatoday.com.

19 The New York Times, October 13,2022, *Jeffrey Clark Was Considered Unassuming. Then He Plotted With Trump.* By Katie Benner and Charlie Savage.

20 https://www.forbes.com/micholasreimann. "Arizona Audit Cost Trump Supporters Nearly $6 Million – Only to Assert Biden Won By Even More." Written by Nicholas Reimann, Forbes. September24, 2021.

21 https://www.washingtonpost.com/world/2022. "Long Before His War in Ukraine, Putin Waged War on Russian Media."

22 The Washington Post, September 24, 2002, Robyn Dixon.

23 Ibid.

24 The New York Times, "Putin Defends Police Raid on Media Company.", by Celestine Bohlen.

25 Ibid.

26 https://en.wikipedia.org/wiki/list of journalists killed."

27 The Committee to Protect Journalists (CP), July 2000.

28 Ibid.

29 https://lrp.fas.org/world/russia/fsb/history. The Federal Security Service began on April 3, 1995.

30 Dugin, Alekandr, The Foundations of Geopolitics, Moscow, Russia, 1997.

31 https://www.reuters.com "Campaign of Fear, The Trump world's assault on U.S. election workers."

32 https://www/wsws/prg. October 2, 2022, "Trump Issues Death Threat targeting Republican Senator Mitch McConnell," by Jacob Crosse.

33 https://www.bbc.com, "Trump sides with Russia against FBI at Helsinki Summit," July 16, 2018.

34 https://www.cnn.com/trump/putin/summit/cnnphotos, 2018/07/18.

35 The Washington Post, July 17, 2018.

36 www.npr.com, July 17, 2018.

37 *Russian Roulette*, Michael Isikoff and David Corn, Page ix.

38 *Russian Roulette*, Michael Isikoff and David Corn, page x.

39 https://apnews.com, April 15, 1987, by Bryan Brumley.

40 Ibid.

41 Indian Aerospace Defence News, June 13, 2018.

42 Punch Agency Report, "President Trump caught 'on tape' discussing payment to prostitute, NYT Claims."

43 https://www.nbcnews.com "Jeffrey Epstein introduced me to Trump at 14, Ghislaine Mazxwell accuser says. Testifying at the Maxwell's trial in New York City, the woman, identified by the pseudonym Jane, said she met the former president in the 1990s at his Mar-a-Lago resort." by Tom Winter and Corky Siemaszko, December 1, 2021.

44 https://www.nytimes.com/interative/donald-trump-taxes.

45 https://wwwreuters.com "Russian Elite Invested nearly $100 million in Trump buildings," March 17, 2017.

46 https://washingtonpost.com/world/2019/10/04.

47 https://investmentpolicy.unctag.org/measures/russia. "Expands the list of sectors strategic for national security for the Russian Federation."

48 Ibid.

49 https://elbasy.kz – An important channel of distribution and explaining the main trends of political and socio-economic programs of Kazakhstan.

50 The Tolkuchka Bazaar outside of Ashgabat was considered one of the largest in the world, and sold not only beautiful handmade rugs, but antiques, cars, food, camels, sheep, clothes, artwork, paintings, and other items. I could go there early in the morning and spend an entire Saturday or Sunday negotiating prices with sellers. I brought back to the U.S. several large rugs.

51 https://www.cnn.com. "Afghan prison ordeal ends happily for US aid workers." November 2003.

52 *Prisoners of Hope*, written by Dayna Curry and Heather Mercer, WaterBrook Press, December 18, 2003.

53 https://en.wikipedia.org/wiki/Sapamurat_Niyazov, also known as Turkmenbashi, who ruled Turkmenistan from 1985 to 2006.

54 https://wwwwashingtonpost.comn. "Why did Trump send federal agents to Portland?", July 07, 2020.

55 Ibid.

56 https://www.washingtonpost.com, "Trump threatens to deploy federal agents to Chicago and other U.S. cities led by Democrats," by Nick Miroff and Mark Berman, The Washington Post, July 20, 2020.

57 https://www.reuters.com, "Factbox: Afghan cities taken over by the Taliban," August 15, 2021.

58 https://www.theatlantic.com, "Donald Trump and the Politics of Fear" – The Atlantic, September 2, 2016.

59 https;//www.cdc.gov. "CDC reports the first laboratory-confirmed case of the 2019 Novel Coronavirus in the U.S. from samples taken on January 19 in Washington State." Reported on January 20, 2020.

60 https://www.businessinsider.com, "Trump Dismissed Coronavirus Warnings in January 2020." June 30, 2021.

61 CNBC, May 18, 2020, by Berkeley Lovelace Jr and Kevin Breuninger, "Trump says he takes hydroxychloroquine to prevent coronavirus infection even though it's an unproven treatment. A small study in Brazil was halted for safety reasons after coronavirus patients taking chloroquine, which hydroxdychloroquine is derived from, developed arrhythmia (heart problems including some who died.")

62 https://www.washingtonpost.com, "Southeast U.S. poised for a firestorm of omicron cases, with few safeguards in place." The Washington Post, 2022/01/02.

63 CNN/Interviews in Alabama, March 2021.

64 https://apnews.com, "Trump wears mask in public for the first time during pandemic," July 11, 2020.

65 The World Health Organization, COVID-19 Dashboard of Cases and Deaths, https://covid19.who.int.

66 Ibid.

67 Ibid.

68 The Washington Post, 5/10/2021, reported by Jessica Lipscomb.

69 https://washingtonpost.com, 2022/09/07 "Ron DeSantis and the worst fallacy about vaccine skepticism."

70 https://www.washingtonpost.com, "The Health 2020: Doctors, hospitals blast Trump's baseless claims that they inflate coronavirus deaths for money." November 3, 2020.

71 https://www.ncbi.nlm.nih.gov. "Death by political party: The relationship between COVID-19 deaths and political party affiliation in the United States." Written by Benjamin Radford and Jinging Gao, June 13, 2021.

72 https://www.haaretz.com_U.S.News. "America is losing Its 'Leader of the Free World' Mantle. America's designated leadership of the Free World is less about its foreign commitments and more about its sorry internal state of the union. For the past five years (during Trump), the U.S. has been regarded as a 'flawed democracy.' Unless it can resolve its internal problems, the rest of the world will lose faith in American leadership." Written by Alon Pinkas, July 25, 2021.

Chapter One

Standing Up To Racism

R ace is one of the most volatile issues in our society and one of the most difficult to deliberate or discuss. This book attempts to examine the U.S. variety of racism and discrimination from a distinctive and global perspective.

Because I am a White woman, my opinions are what they are, yet also unique. I have lived in cultures and other countries for an extended period where I WAS the minority race. I have intimately observed and absorbed the horrors of genocide (Rwanda) and an ethnic cleansing war (Bosnia) – both caused by racism, ethnic strife, and hatred. I grew up during the civil rights era of the sixties. I have examined U.S. racism through adversarial eyes for more than twenty years abroad, where I felt the disdain for my homeland from other cultures precisely due to this issue.

Any discourse about racism in America needs to provide a tool for each of us to earnestly measure our own habits and thoughts regarding this issue. The conversation must begin – whether it's internal or with friends and family. We can no longer deny that racism is a type of cruel pathology embedded deeply within thought processes - a product of fear, hatred, and perhaps ignorance. This hatred is destroying our country. We are ALL Americans, and our diversity is a strength and the very backbone of the United States. If we collectively do not resolve this issue relatively soon, there may not be a United States much longer.

The prevailing view of racism in the U.S. is complicated, and there is a different definition and reaction on every corner of every neighborhood. No matter who is discussing this issue, it remains the basis for segregation, discrimination, biases, blind brutality, and even cold-blooded murder. Denial of racism by many White individuals in the U.S. is commonplace, but this current wave of "Black Lives Matters" and the death of George Floyd has forced some of these biased individuals to re-exam their consciences. This means that a small open crack may exist in these previously closed minds.

Robin DiAngelo wrote *White Fragility* a book about "Why it's so hard for White People to Talk about Racism." I highly recommend this book for anyone who truly wants to understand their own reaction to this subject. The following is a short excerpt:

Race is an evolving social idea that was created to legitimize racial in-equality and protect White advantage. The term "White" first appeared in colonial law in the late 1600s. By 1790, people were asked to claim their race on the census, and by 1825, the perceived degrees of blood determined who would be classified as Indian. From the late 1800s through the early twentieth century, as waves of immigrants entered the United States, the concept of a White race was solidified.

People of color, including W.E.B. Du Bois and James Balwin, have been writing about Whiteness for decades... These writers urged White people to turn their attention onto themselves to explore what it means to be White in a society that is so divided by race. For example, a French reporter asked expatriate writer Richard White his thoughts on the "Negro problem" in the United States. White replied, "There isn't any Negro problem; there is only a White problem. As White pointed out, racism against people of color doesn't occur in a vacuum."

There is no need to present an organized didactic defining "racism" or discuss whether racism exists in the United States. Of course it does. In fact, racism in America is alive and living deep within the psyche of many, and perhaps the majority of our White citizens. Those who don't recognize it are either naïve or in denial. Racism is historically linked with slavery because the two issues evolved together in the U.S. In this respect, the American experience is distinctive.

Robin DiAngelo continued her eloquent writing by saying:

As a White person, I can openly and unabashedly reminisce about "the good ole days." Claiming that the past was socially better than the present is a hallmark of White privilege, which manifests itself in the ability to remain oblivious to our racial history. Claiming that the past was socially better than the present is also a hallmark of White supremacy. Consider any period in the past from the perspective of people of color: 246 years of brutal enslavement; the rape of Black women for the pleasure of White men and to produce more enslaved workers; the selling off of Black children; the attempted genocide of Indigenous people, Indian removal acts, and reservations; indentured servitude, lynching, and mob violence; share-cropping; Chinese exclusion laws; Japanese American internment; Jim Crow laws of mandatory segregation; Black codes; bans on Black jury service; bans on voting; imprisoning people for unpaid work; medical sterilization and experimentation; employment discrimination; educational discrimination; inferior schools; biased laws and policing practices; redlining and subprime mortgages; mass incarceration; racist media representations; cultural erasures, attacks, and mockery; and untold and perverted historical accounts. You can now see how a romanticized past is strictly a White construct. But it is a powerful construction because it calls out to a deeply internalized sense of superiority and entitlement and the sense that any advancement for people of color is an encroachment on this entitlement."

"Equal or Better Than", Artist – Pat Byrnes, Courtesy of Cagle Cartoons.

History of Racism in America

History is always relevant, and without understanding how we arrived at today's high rate of law enforcement-related deaths of people of Color, we cannot purport to discuss how to improve justice in the U.S.

In the late eighteenth century, the United States became a free society, inspired by the words "all men are created equal and endowed by their Creator with certain inalienable rights." [1] Jefferson was a slave owner at the time he wrote those words in our Declaration of Independence.[2] The hypocrisy of this lie has been continued in our country for centuries. It was not easy to justify slavery for a society revolting in the name of liberty and equality. Yet many Americans found a way to settle this contradiction, and eventually, the Supreme Court Dred Scott decision of 1857 was written, pronouncing slave ownership as a fundamental property right.[3]

It would take more than a hundred years to rectify this wrongful decision. The doctrine that slaves were legally comparable to property generated both legal and human rebuttals, especially concerning White slave owners having sex with their slaves – considered bestiality.[4]

Leap forward to the Marxist rationalization of racism. Karl Marx lived from 1818 to 1883[5] and is best known for his 1848 publication called the *Manifest of the Communist Party*. He believed that the concept of "racial superiority existed to explain civilizational differences and was therefore amalgamated in America to justify continuing racial subjugation. Thus, as far back as the mid-1800's, began the Soviet explanation of American-style Black discrimination and racism. The difference is that Karl Marx's racist reasoning was based on economic defenses, whereby the reality of U.S. racism was based more on moral justifications for the inhumanity of slavery."[6] This sick form of American racism has been handed down from fathers to sons, within families, and over countless generations to the point that many Whites today (2022) do not even understand their own thoughts on this topic. It is just ingrained and accepted.

No mention of racism in the United States is relative without discussing the 1921 Tulsa, Oklahoma massacre.[7] This massacre puts American racism on the scale of other global racial conflicts. Basically, in June 1921, a White mob went to the Greenwood District of Tulsa, Oklahoma, and murdered over three hundred Black residents – men, women, and children. It was perhaps the largest and most vile case of racial violence/murder in the United States, but there are so many other examples that shame and dishonor our country.

The 1960's era was turbulent for those of us who experienced the assassinations of President John Kennedy, Martin Luther King Jr., and then Robert Kennedy. I still remember sitting in the northern California undercover office of the CIA - my father's office - when the news announced the death of President Kennedy. People across our nation were glued to their TV screens and watched the incomprehensible shooting, death and funeral of our President. I was in my late teens and still a dreamer and a pragmatist. When Martin Luther King Jr. was shot, the "idealist view of America" radically changed for many. I was among those who no longer viewed the U.S. in the same manner. There was rioting, more shooting, and civil unrest, and of course, the "flower children" in San Francisco.[8]

It was King who advocated the nonviolent revolution which resulted in the Civil Rights Act of 1964, the Voting Rights Act of 1965, and the Fair Housing laws of 1968.[9] The principle of these laws was nondiscrimination. However, King's progress was cut short due to his assassination. Even the removal of some legal barriers to racial discrimination didn't generate the outcomes expected. The fabric of American-style democracy had been slashed, and no one or nothing could repair it. Race discrimination prevailed in most areas, especially throughout the South. In reality, very little changed.

In the 1990s Dinesh D'Souza wrote in his book *The End of Racism*,[10]

"Racism therefore, flourished in the interregnum between the principles of the (American) Constitution and its pragmatic concession to the institution of slavery. Far from being proof of distinctive American evil, racism is a peculiar reflection of the moral conscience of America and of the West. It reflects the oppressor's need to account for the betrayal of his highest ideals.[11]

Fortunately, the "oppressors" (slave owners) of early American history have all died and, along with them their grotesque sense of idealism. What has since been passed down within generations of Americans is actually a distinctive American immoral, illogical form of loathing and hatred toward other human beings. It is, without a doubt, proof of a distinctive American evil.

"Evil Forces in the USA," Artist – Paresh Nath, Courtesy of Cagle Cartoons.

In 1993, thousands of people, mostly African-Americans, gathered on the nation's Capital Mall on the thirtieth anniversary of the original King March and his "*I Have a Dream*" speech. It was evident that the King dream of meaningful equality had not been realized by the 1990s.[12]

A member of the Martin Luther King Jr. team was a young man named John Robert Lewis. As an American civil rights leader, he was primarily known for his involvement in the "Bloody Sunday" March that took place in Selma, Alabama in 1965. His entire adult life was dedicated to fighting discrimination. Beginning in 1987, he served seventeen terms in the U.S. House of Representatives. John Lewis died of cancer in July 2020.

"To thunderous applause at the (John Lewis) funeral service at Ebenezer Baptist Church, former President Obama summoned the names of Southern segregationists of the 1960s to make a point about how little has changed when it comes to protesters standing up against the government to right what they perceive as injustice."[13] He said, "Bull Conner may be gone, but today we witness with our own eyes police officers kneeling on the back of Black Americans. George Wallace may be gone, but we can witness our federal government (Trump)

sending agents to use tear gas and batons on peaceful and legal demonstrators."
14

His Eulogy was eloquent and the speech that I had been waiting for him to say during his presidency. Our country's leaders must spearhead this effort dealing with the repulsive face of racism and rally others, not just Blacks, to revolutionize our society. No one is more qualified to lead this charge than former President Obama. When Obama was elected President of the United States, the whole world applauded. Many nations believed his election was a sign that the U.S. had finally resolved inequality, racial tensions, and violence. Unfortunately, Obama was primarily burdened with resolving a nationwide financial fiasco, potential economic collapse, and one catastrophe after another which consumed his time and attention. He is now focused on American youth, but it is still not too late for him to consider and participate in resolutions to our country's racial tensions. While working with American youth is admirable and needed – our country cannot wait for them to step up and lead. This problem needs immediate attention and tomorrow is already too late – another young Black man will die. Tyre Nichols (Date of Death: January 10, 2023)[15] was only 29 years old when he was beat to death by five Memphis police officers. How many more Black men must be killed until President Obama speaks up or until our country and our government officials step up and stop this insanity.

Both Blacks and Whites respect and listen to former President Obama. His articulate and persuasive speeches impacted the minds of most Americans - a critical trait to help heal racism in America. More importantly, our country is under attack by Putin and racism is one of the weapons exploited. Putin manipulates racism to create more violence and destruction in our democracy. It divides our citizens instead of bonding our society and country. We need UNITY now!

When President Obama announced to the nation that Osama bin Laden had been found and killed – all Americans cheered and there was a sense of united nationality across our country. [16]

After Obama, Trump became president. He not only did not respond to the police murders of our Black citizens, but commented that the KKK are "fine people." This was reported by The Atlantic on 8/15/2017 that "Trump Defends White Nationalist Protesters by calling them fine people."[17] My initial response to Trump's words was "OMG".

Not long after King's death, Malcolm X stepped up with his motto of "Black is Beautiful."[18] Unfortunately, his approach to further the Black cause (the term Black replaced the term Negro as an acceptable label during the Malcolm X timeframe) was to fight back rather than use peaceful demonstrations. The Black Power salute was attributed to Malcolm X and because of his efforts, discrimination was mostly outlawed from numerous societal sectors. "While his methods were the opposite of MLK Jr. his time in the public eye resulted in some level of positive outcomes."[19]

D'Souzza said in his book *The End of Racism*, "this era was followed by an outbreak of riots across the U.S. starting in the Watts area of Los Angeles and spreading to Detroit and elsewhere, the revolts seemed to turn previously tranquil areas into cauldrons of violence."[20] Los Angeles erupted in anger and fire after the brutal police attack on Rodney King.[21] Four policemen were acquitted despite the fact that their savage beating of King was video recorded and then broadcast into homes across the country and even abroad. This was another example of how our democracy failed.

In 1991, I was living in Moscow, Russia. The Rodney King beating and the subsequent fires, looting, and riots were televised in Russia along with articles and photos in local Russian newspapers. This provided authentication to Russians – and others worldwide - that the United States was a lawless country and a violent civilization. College courses in Russia today still teach the inherent moral evil of American slavery and its continuing, lingering aftermath of unconscious bias, underlying prejudices, and police brutality. These same college textbooks were educating Russians about the Tulsa massacre many years before the rest of the U.S. populace learned that about three hundred Black people had been slaughtered by an angry White mob – a form of ethnic cleansing comparable to what happened in Bosnia or even Rwanda.

Is the United States any different than Bosnia or Rwanda? Could a civil or ethnic cleansing war break out? In 2022-2023 we have the state of Texas, assisted by the state of Florida, shipping unassuming migrants and refugees to New York City and abandoning them on New York City streets.[22] Note that both Texas and Florida have Republican Governors while New York has a Democratic Governor.

The Tulsa massacre was almost a century ago, yet in 2021 the same type of angry White mob attempted to destroy the U.S. Capitol building and overthrow our country's legal election.[23] There is nothing more sacred to a democracy than elections. This violent, crazed crowd assaulted the Capitol Police and searched for former Vice President Pence yelling "hang Mike Pence" in order to murder him on the steps of the Capitol building.[24] Most news sources say that five people died in the Capitol Riot – one police officer, a rioter was shot, and three others died during the rampage – with over one hundred police officers injured.[25]

Current Racism in America

So, where are we as a society? What, if anything, has changed? What it feels like is that the hatred and racism in the U.S. has intensified so that the isolated lynching(s) of yesteryear are now the more public police murders of today. Racial hatred and outright murder have become more preponderate and customary. It was slavery and the concept of racial domination in the U.S. that led to today's underlying prejudices, unconscious biases, all-consuming hatred, and eventually to police brutality. The death of so many young Black men in the U.S., including George Floyd, is a harsh example of the state of the Union in the year 2020.[26] Curtis Bunn wrote: "According to data collected by *The Washington Post*, police shot and killed at least 1,055 people nationwide last year (2021), the most since the newspaper began tracking fatal shootings by officers in 2015. Blacks, who account for 13 percent of the U.S. population, accounted for 27 percent of those fatally shot and killed by police in 2021."[27]

But in the microcosm of time, the death of George Floyd has shown a heroic surge towards the principles of nondiscrimination. Gianna, his seven-year-old daughter (2021), believes that her daddy changed the world.[28] Let's hope so.

What is the American version of racism, and how/why is it so ingrained and customary in our law enforcement agencies that our news and media report a police shooting or killing of an African-American citizen DAILY? The police officer who killed George Floyd is Derek Chauvin. During his murder trial and a few weeks before and after (about twenty days), there were sixty-four police-involved shootings of a person of Color in the United States as reported by the *New York Times* on November 30, 2021. Yes, you read that right – not one or two - but sixty-four shootings! These victims are human beings who were shot, hurt, and killed by police hatred and violence. Passing legislation and the Police Reform Bill is a start, but just like other legislation passed in Congress to fight discrimination – it is not the solution to change the hearts and minds of Americans who are committing these murders.

Social marketing methodologies and messaging convinced most Americans to stop smoking or to buckle-up for safety when driving, therefore a nationwide strong social marketing campaign must begin and be funded by Congress, to transform racists and transition our society. Mind changing techniques – denouncing hatred and violence and explaining the need for equality - need to be implemented and employed - THEN enforced by new legislation, compulsory throughout our nation, and punishable with jail or prison time.

If we want our societies to stop feeding off hatred, then they must have a substitution that will satisfy their souls.

"George Floyd Anniversary Local Toon", Artist – Steve Sack, Courtesy of Cagle Cartoons

Fatal Encounters[29] is a public site that aims to document all episodes of fatal police-civilian interactions in the U.S.[30] It includes homicides, suicides, accidental deaths, and all cases are fact-checked against published accounts before being added to the public data set. The site is run by D. Brian Burghart, a former editor and publisher of the Reno News and Review, and a journalism instructor at the University of Nevada in Reno.[31] This website shows an average of 1,028 deaths per year or about three incidents per day of police-involved deaths of persons of Color.[32]

So I ask you, the White audience reading this book, what would you feel like if you were mistaken for a person of color during a police confrontation? You could be wearing a hoodie, a mask, and sunglasses. What if you were too tanned in the summer? What would need to happen to make you sympathetic or more compassionate toward others?

D. L. Hughley wrote a book titled *How to Survive America*. The following quote is from his "Introduction."

Black and Brown folks are in a battle for survival every damn day in this country, in a way white people can't fully comprehend. . . . Our life-expectancy is a full three years less than white Americans. The very air we breathe is more polluted, our water is more contaminated, our local food options are toxic, and our jobs are underpaid.

Folks where I grew up in South Central L.A. aren't jogging to the local Whole Foods for a smoothie. Even if they could afford it, odds are they'd have early stage lung cancer by the time they got there. . . According to the American Cancer Society, African Americans have the highest death rate from most cancers and the lowest survival length. Our kidneys fail us at three times the rate of Whites . . . Our communities are statistically less safe than the average, and yes we're terrorized by law-enforcement and the criminal justice systems that are supposed to protect us, instead they are sending us to prison at five times the rate of Whites.

It is the White population in the United States that needs to adjust their hateful attitudes, but for our society to revolutionize and change, all of us must work together and understand each other – White, Brown, Black, and all others.

White society is NOT superior to Black society – we are all humans. It was primarily a White mob that just violently attacked the Capitol in January 2021. It was a White President that sent federal troops to beat and gas people participating in legal and peaceful demonstrations in Portland, Oregon and again in Washington, D.C.[33] He then organized a violent and armed crowd to attack the U.S. Capitol and stop the legal transfer of power in a legal election.[34] Plain and simple – Trump broke the law and should be tried and convicted just like any other citizen of this country.

Do you remember the photos of firefighters, police, and other heroes all working at the 9-11 New York site after the Twin Towers collapsed? Everyone was covered in soot – regardless of race, color, or even gender.[35] Each person looked indistinguishable from the person standing next to them and they were all the identical color of dirty gray. It took the worst incident of international terrorism in the United States to implant the impression that all these Americans were similar – just ordinary people trying to survive a disaster.

The Dellums Commission and the Joint Center for Political and Economic Studies, Health Policy Institute in Washington, D.C., requested a report from James B. Hyman, Ph.D. on "Men and Communities: African American Males and the Well-Being of Children, Families, and Neighborhoods . . ." He initiates this paper by saying, "Before we begin this discussion, it must be acknowledged that this is a sensitive topic and, for some readers, perhaps even an explosive one." In the conclusion, he states, "Hence... (Many) would argue that racism in the U.S. is the greatest determinant of the influence that Black men have on the well-being of their children, families, and neighborhoods... Finding practicable policy and programmatic vehicles to remedy or perhaps neutralize the impacts of racism would clearly alter the opportunity structure for Blacks in ways that could offer immeasurable well-being consequences. Unfortunately, this has not been achieved to-date." [36] This report was written in 2005.

As of July 2020, three Minneapolis police officers charged in connection with the death of George Floyd face criminal charges while mourners said goodbye to the man whose death ignited more than a month of national and international demonstrations and protests. J. Alexander Kueng, Thomas Lane, and Tou Thao, were each charged with one count of aiding and abetting second-degree murder and aiding and abetting second-degree manslaughter. The Hennepin County Attorney's Office charged Derek Chauvin with third-degree murder and second-degree manslaughter.[37] He was eventually convicted on all counts and sentenced to more than twenty-two years in prison.[38] We can expect another round of warranted protests if any of the other men are acquitted, as happened in the Rodney King police beating or the Breona Taylor police murder. Will these criminal charges change racism in the United States? It is a start, but NOT THE FINAL RESOLUTION.

U.S. citizens need to connect the dots between police murders of our Black citizens, the raging hatred and violence perpetrated by White supremacists and others, the mass murders and shootings in almost every state, Trump's speeches filled with dishonest information and his disdain for minorities, and the lack of cooperation between our elected officials. We need to view the bigger picture while understanding "why" our country is so violent and hateful. It is time for major changes.

The vicious concept of "white supremacy" has only thrived in Germany and the United States. We all know what happened in Germany, but the "White Supremacy" Trump-following domestic terrorists demonstrated their Trump-led heated and blind fury on January sixth when they stormed the U.S. Capitol building. These people were brainwashed and molded into a murderous, caustic, violent, and destructive state of mind. It is a form of radicalization. Hitler used the same methodologies to influence the minds of an entire country which resulted in horrific mass murders of millions of people throughout Europe. This should be a "wakeup call" to the United States – we are moving in this same direction.

Cartoon Caption: "Whole Lotta Love," Artist – Bruce Plante, Courtesy of Cagle Cartoons

Shortly after January sixth, the FBI issued a public statement that "White supremacy individuals were the biggest threat to U.S. democracy."[39] I agree with this FBI public statement. However, to resolve the White supremacy growing threat there needs to be a nationwide identification of the cause. This means the "minds" of these individuals must change. As a threat to our nation this group of violent and hate-filled individuals have weaponized mind manipulation so that their brains primarily respond to negative chemistry. If they are physically removed from the daily influx of hate-filled messages from their colleagues, their brains and thoughts may change over time. Does this mean serving prison time or is there an alternative? Some of the Capitol rioters apologized in court, but does that mean their minds have become less violent or destructive?[40]

"The FBI investigates terrorism, counterintelligence, cyber-crime, public corruption, civil rights, organized crime, white-collar crime, violent crime, and more. In their Counterintelligence division, they say "Spies might seem like a throwback to earlier days of world wars and cold wars, but they are more common than ever – and they are targeting our nation's most valuable secrets. The FBI is the lead agency for exposing, preventing, and investigating intelligence activities in the U.S. Because much of today's spying is accomplished by data theft from computer networks, espionage is quickly becoming cyber-based."[41] The majority of these cyber-attacks come from Russia.

Furthermore, the strife and discord found in every city in the U.S. were most likely foreseen by President Putin. While it was Trump's character, decisions and speeches that instigated this growing divide between our citizens, government, and political parties, it was probably Putin who planted the seeds or provided Trump with instructions.[42] Another possibility is that Trump and/or his family had been threatened by Putin or another Russian working for Putin. Because of Trump's drastic illegal steps to remain as the President of the United States, I believe Putin warned Trump of the potential lethal consequences if he failed.

The burning question is: did Putin compromise Trump with Russian prostitutes when Trump was in Moscow; is Trump indebted to Putin or other Russians due to his borrowing of large sums of money to finance his businesses; or is Trump responding to Putin's suggestions because he wants a Trump Tower in Moscow? In any one of these scenarios, there is no doubt in my mind that Putin is and has been running the show – not just in Russia, but in the U.S (especially with Trump in the White House) the U.K., France, Germany and other nations.

Putin intends to destroy democracy from within – and he is succeeding. His tools used to achieve his goals are – racism, violence, antisemitism, insurrection, cyberattacks, inflation, brainwashing, and isolation. He believes in the philosophy of "divide and conquer" and nowhere is this more evident than in the U.S. two-party government system of Democrats vs. Republicans. He has used American isolationism to harm the U.S. and plant the seeds of hatred and violence. Due to this, our citizens often do not know what is happening in their daily lives or why. They don't know who to trust. This is especially true in rural America – where information spreads by word-of-mouth (by friends) rather than factual statistics and truths. If you look at an election map – these rural areas are usually red.

How do I know this? I lived under Communism in the Soviet Union, then Russia, and Central Asia long enough to become bi-cultural. This means that I learned to think, behave, and look, Russian. I resided in a Russian apartment, and over time became just another Russian on the streets of Moscow and other cities.[43]

To think like a Russian does not happen if you just study the language. While working at Science Applications International Corporation (SAIC) in Colorado, I was required to learn to read and correct technical Russian. We had the largest Russian-language military, technical, and intelligence library in the United States. I attended Russian language classes three to four days a week for several years. Every night after I helped my four children do their homework, I had my own homework to complete. I could edit our transliterated Russian-language database of material after one year of Russian studies. During this timeframe, I also studied about the Russian culture and lifestyle.

This prepared me for actually living in Russia, for conversing with others, or for understanding how to daily survive. It took another two to three years of everyday exposure to Russian society before I felt totally comfortable catching a ride on the street, for conducting business transactions, for conversing with other Russians for hours while sitting in the Radisson lobby sipping wine, or for buying or negotiating grocery prices in the open markets throughout Moscow, St. Petersburg, Smolensk, and other cities. More importantly, I learned to "think" and "reason" as any other Russian. While I was still considered a "foreigner" by many that I met, my language skills were good enough that I was often asked whether I was from the "Baltics" and not the U.S. – a different speech accent. Eventually, at a large conference for Russian orphans held in St. Petersburg, I was the guest speaker to the hundreds who attended. I was introduced by Boris Alchuster as "one of us" – perhaps the greatest compliment that I ever received and affirmation that I had indeed become bi-cultural.

The Russian Government is more predictable than the U.S. Government. Every man or woman on a street in Russia – including myself – usually understands Putin and his motivations and actions. In Russia, Putin is the sole decision-maker, while in the U.S. the Will of the people and of the Congress contributes to just about every political decision.

Putin's tolerance for dissidents is greater than Trump's, but once he wishes to eliminate an individual, he does. Trump, on the other hand, once mentioned via Twitter that "protestors should be shot," [44] and his impatience for anyone less than one hundred percent loyal to him was exhibited often by the massive number of people who left his employment – either voluntarily or who were terminated.[45] Trump's wrath was exhibited daily, but somehow our democracy prevailed.

While living in Russia, I was the senior manager of several nonprofit organizations that worked primarily with U.S. Government multi-million-dollar grants. In Russia, those working with me were almost entirely Russian. Russian employees do not question or oppose their employers. There is an unspoken level of respect that appears lost in the United States. As the senior manager, I often received advice but never received opposition. After I returned to the U.S. and was the Chief Executive of a large non-profit in Chicago, I found that everyone questioned everything. This is a sacred right of living in a democracy, however I miss the everyday respect for each other found in Russia.

What needs to be understood by every U.S. citizen is that both men – Putin and Trump – want absolute power. Putin has this power, and very, very few people in Russia oppose him. Trump did not have this power because the U.S. is a democracy – a concept that Trump did not seem to grasp. So instead of accepting that he lost the election fairly, he instigated a violent riot and inspired people to attack the U.S. Capitol and our elected officials.

For most of 2022, the "Select Congressional Committee to Investigate the Attack on the U.S. Capitol"[46] regularly met and then published a detailed report with the assistance of The New York Times. This report states that "as Mr. Trump worked to overturn the election, he was told repeatedly – including by his own Justice Department – that his claims are false." This attack on the Capitol was Mr. Trump's desperate last ditch effort to stop the transfer of power.

Even more hideous is that the many Republicans in Congress, including Mitch McConnell, began "damage control" and attempted to cover-up this attack on the Capitol.

"GOP Blocks Capitol Riot Commission", Artist – Dave Whamond, Courtesy of Cagle Cartoons.

In fact, Trump's actions were comparable to President Yeltsin in Russia when he staged the coup. The Russian Parliament was attempting to restrict Yeltsin's presidential powers, so his military tanks fired heavy artillery into the Parliament building (the Russian White House). This vicious event, just like Trump's attack on the U.S. Capitol, was due to over-sized bruised egos in response to not getting what they wanted.

In Trump's case, there were other circumstantial reasons as well – such as the possibility that his life or the lives of his family could have been threatened. As long as Trump is of use to Putin and Russia, he is relatively safe. Even if Trump is not the President of the United States, as long as he has real estate and a multi-million dollar business – the Russians can use him and his businesses to channel black cash into the United States. In fact, of all the crimes committed by Donald Trump – his real estate businesses are most useful to Russia and should be investigated.

Once Trump lost the election, the reality of Russian threats increased. This was the same timeframe that Ivana Trump died from a blunt-blow to her head[47] – reportedly due to a fall down her apartment steps. I seriously doubt that her death was an accident.

CHAPTER 1 – END NOTES

1 https://www.archives.gov/declaration_transription. Originally published July 4, 1776.

2 https://monticello.org. "But the Declaration did not extend "Life, Liberty, and the pursuit of Happiness" to African Americans, indentured servants, or women. Twelve of the first eighteen American presidents owned slaves. Thomas Jefferson drafted the Declaration and called slavery an 'abominable crime', yet he was a lifelong slaveholder."

3 https://www.sos.mo.gov. "Missouri's Dred Scott Case, 1846 – 1857… in it's 1857 decision that stunned the nation, the United States Supreme Court upheld slavery in the United States …"

4 https://journals.psu.edu. "Things Fearful to Name": Bestiality in Colonial America. Written by John M. Murrin.

5 https://monthlyreview.org/July1, 2020. "Central to Marx's treatment of modern slavery was the recognition of the absolutely horrific nature of slaveowner capitalism, which (in his thoughts) made it worse than all other forms of slavery known in history.

6 Tome Boromore (Editor), *Karl Marx*, C.A. Watts and company, Ltd, McGraw-Hill Book Company, Englewood Cliffs, N.J. Copyright 1956.

7 https://www.tulsahistory.org., Tulsa Historical Society and Museum, a website of events.

8 https://www.pinterest.com. "18 Photos of Haight Street Hippies, San Francisco in 1967."

9 https://www.history.com/topics/black-history. The Civil Rights Acts of 1964, 1965, and 1968.

10 The End of Racism, The Free Press, New York, N.Y., 1995, p. 84.

11 Ibid.

12 https://kinginstitute.stanford.edu.

13 https://www.nytimes.com. "President Barak Obama's Eulogy for John Lewis: Full Transcript.

14 Ibid.

15 https://www.businessinsider.com. "Tyre Nichols Death: Timneline of Arrest, Death, from being stopped by Memphis cops to officers being charged with his murder." Written by Sinead Baker, Michelle Mark, Lloyd Lee, Haven Orecchio-Egresitz, and Yelena Dzhanova, January 31, 2023.

16 https://obamawhitehouse.archives.gov. "Osama Bin Laden Dead, Summary: President Obama addresses the Nation to announce that the United States has killed Osama bin Laden, the leader of al Qaeda." Written by Macon Phillips, May 2, 2011.

17 The Atlantic, August 15, 2017, "Trump Defends White Nationalist Protesters by calling them 'fine people."

18 https://biography.com/activist/malcom-X. "Malcolm X – Quotes, Movie & Children – A Biography." Feb. 12, 2015.

19 Christ for the Nations, "Why Do the Righteous Suffer?" January 1, 1976.

20 The End of Racism, The Free Press, New York, N.Y., 1995.

21 Ibid.

22 https://www.cnn.com, "Texas is sending migrants to New York and Washington, D.C.", August 19, 2022.

23 https://npr.org, "A Capitol Police Officer injured on January 6th Recalls the Chaos and Carnage.", June 9, 2022.

24 https://www.newyorker.com/News/Capitol-Riot, "The Devastating New History of the January 6th Insurrection, December 22, 2022.

25 https://www.nytimes.com, "These Are the 5 People Who Died in the Capitol Riot." October 13, 2022.

26 https://www.nbcnews.com, "Report: Black people are still killed by police at a higher rate than other groups." Written by Curtis Bunn, March 3, 2022.

27 Ibid.

28 ET News, "George Floyd's Daughter Gianna Declares 'Daddy Changed the World' in a Moving Clip, Written by Rachel McRady, june 3, 2020, 4:26 AM PDT.

29 https://www.fatelencounters.org.

30 Ibid.

31 Ibid.

32 Ibid.

33 https://en.wikipedia.org, "2020 Deployment of Federal Troops in the United States In June 2020." In June 2020, the Trump administration began deploying federal law enforcement forces to select cities in the United States in response to rioting and . . . "

34 The January 6 Report, Findings From the Select Committee to Investigate the Attack on the U.S. Capitol," Published by The New York Times.

35 https://www.washingtonpost.com. September 11: The famous photo of 'Dust Lady' Marcy still haunts us after all these years." September 11, 2018.

36 "Men and Communities: African American Males and the Well-Being of Children, Families, and Neighborhoods." Background Paper for the Joint Center Health Policy Institute, 2005, written by Dr. James Hyman.

37 https://www.ag.state.mn.us. Office of Attorney General Keith Ellison, March 11, 2021. Eventually, Chauvin pleaded guilty to third-degree murder charge.

38 https://npr.org. "Derek Chauvin is Sentenced to 22 ½ Years for George Floyd's murder." June 25, 2021.

39 FBI Director, Christopher Wray, testifying in front of the Senate Judiciary Committee on Tuesday, 3/3/2021.

40 https://www.pbs.org." Some Capitol rioters apologize in court for January 6, downplay crimes after." "Appearing before a federal judge after pleading guilty to a felony charge in the deadly Capitol riot, former West Virginia lawmaker Derrick Evans expressed remorse for letting down his family and his community, saying he made a 'crucial mistake. Less than a year later, Evans is portraying himself as a victim of a politically motivated prosecution as he runs to serve in the same building he stormed on January 6, 2021. He describes himself as a 'J6 Patriot." Published on February 3, 2023.

41 https://www.fbi.gov

42 It is this author's opinion that Putin was in control of Trump, the White House, and many aspects of our government's operations from 2018 to 2020. This opinion is based on approximately twelve years of studying Russia and Communism and another twenty years of living and working in Russia and Central Asia.

43 Ibid.

44 https://www.washingtonpost.com/politics/2022/05/02. Written by Philip Bump. "Donald Trump's dangerous view of state violence. "The former president's casual reference to shooting protestors was part..."

45 Brookings Institute, "Tracking turnover in the Trump administration," written by Kathryn Dunn Tempas, January 2021. "President Trump's "A Team" turnover is 92% as of January 20, 2021."

46 The January 6 Report, published by The New York Times, first edition December 2022, p.17.

47 https://www.usatoday.com. "Ivana Trump's death caused by accidental blunt impact injuries," Written by Edward Segarra, USA Today, July 14, 2022.

Chapter Two

Who Really Won The Cold War?

It was only a few decades ago that the Soviet Union and its associated Republics and partner countries encompassed a large portion of the globe. We, the United States, and other "western" nations were their opponents. This resulted in what was coined the Cold War and was a period of geopolitical tensions with a world community living in the shadow of nuclear warfare after World War II and the U.S. nuclear bombing of Japan.[1] This period was a time of rivalry and conflict, primarily between the United States and the Soviet Union.

When former President Reagan met with former Soviet leader Gorbachev, they settled on the terms to end the Cold War and thought it would be in the interest of both countries. However by the time former President George H.W. Bush began his campaign for reelection, he boasted that the U.S. had won the Cold War. This was a slap in the face for Russia. Then Clinton became President and he agreed to expand NATO into the former Warsaw Pact countries (Eastern Europe), which was a violation of the original agreement between Gorbachev and Reagan. Obviously, the U.S. had disregarded the initial negotiated agreement, and therefore Cold War hostilities continued.

When the Soviet Empire collapsed in the early 1990s, the U.S. Government and U.S. citizens believed that the U.S. had won the Cold War. In fact, we had NOT

WON anything, and I have been repeating this since 1993. To demonstrate this fact, we need to fast-forward to the world of 2020 and beyond.

Financial news sources such as The *Economist* and the Bureau of Economic Analysis tell us the cold hard facts in their weekly charts of trade, exchange rates, budget balances, and interest rates. They compare all major countries. In 2018, the trade balance for the United States was a negative $621 billion[2] with imports at $3.1 trillion[3] and exports only $2.5 trillion.[4] Accessed in April 2020, the U.S. International Trade in Goods and Services charts show that 42.1% of the U.S. trade deficit in goods is with China.[5] During this same period, Russia's trade balance was a positive $165.83 billion.[6]

"Another trump casino bankruptcy", Artist – Jimmy Margulies, Courtesy of Cagle Cartoons

An example of pending U.S. economic disaster is that in the 2020 budget year, US revenue total was $3.4 trillion, while spending totaled $4.7 trillion, up almost 49% from a year ago[7]. Thus, our country was well on its way to being the fifth Trump bankruptcy.

Trump's mismanagement of our country's economy was to be expected. He declared bankruptcy four times. Due to this, U.S. banks and other financial institutions refused to loan him more funds. As a result, Trump began doing business with and borrowing money from billionaires in Russia and others in that region.

This list is long and goes back as far as 1990 when Trump met Shalva Tchi-grencky[8]. Catherine Belton wrote in *Putin's People* that "the relationship Tchi-grinsky began to forge with Trump in 1990 would form the roots of a <u>network of Russian intelligence operatives, tycoons and organized-crime associates that has orbited Trump almost ever since</u>."[9] This long list includes: (1) Tamir Sapir from the former Soviet republic of Georgia, (2) Mr. Tevfik Arif from Kazakhstan, and (3) Alexander Mashkevich from Russia. Reportedly, Bayrock was set up by Sater and Arif as a U.S.-based real-estate development firm, and later they were joined by Sapir and Tchigirinsky.[10] They moved into 725 Fifth Ave – a Trump Tower – and one floor below the Trump Organization.[11]

This was not a coincidence. Bayrock and the Russians offered Trump a deal he could not refuse – just like good ole Al Capone. They pay for the financing of several luxury buildings and they would pay Trump a license fee to use his name. Locations included cities like New York, Phoenix, Fort Lauderdale, and others. According to *Putin's People*[12] "more than $98.4 million worth of property in south Florida was bought by Russians in seven Trump-branded luxury towers." Despite Trump tweeting in January 2017 – after he won the election – "I have nothing to do with Russia – no deals, no loans, no nothing"[13] – he did in fact have close ties to many Russians who needed to launder money in the U.S.

Yet Trump has been trading and involved in deals with Russians at least since the 1990's and possibly sooner. Sergei Millian, a former Soviet emigre said on US ABC TV Network that "Trump had made millions of dollars working with Russians."[14] In *Putin's People* page 17, the author states, "The State-owned Sberbank announced it had struck a 'strategic cooperation agreement' with the Crocus Group to finance about 70 percent of a project that would include a tower bearing the Trump name. If the deal went ahead, Trump would officially be doing business in Moscow with the Russian government – in other words working directly for Putin."

What does it mean "working for Putin or with Russians?" It means as a foreigner, you have NO control of the project or the money. Putin, as the leader of a dictatorship country has total manipulation – despite what your signed documents or contracts may say in writing. Putin IS the law, the court, and the final say on all transactions and decisions. Most foreigners do not realize that their "signed contract" is not worth the cost of toilet paper.

The U.S. imports more goods and services than it exports in terms of value and has a trade deficit. By the year 2020, the negative trade balance for the U.S. was $676.7 billion.[15]

Economists use the trade deficit or surplus to measure the relative strength of a country's economy. A country (or anyone) that spends nearly fifty percent more in one year without increasing revenue by the same percentage is heading for disaster. Yet, this is how Trump managed your tax dollars. This is a simple explanation of a complex macroeconomic issue, but it clearly demonstrates Trump's lack of financial management skills, his absence of concern for your tax dollars, and no understanding on how to guide a country's economy.

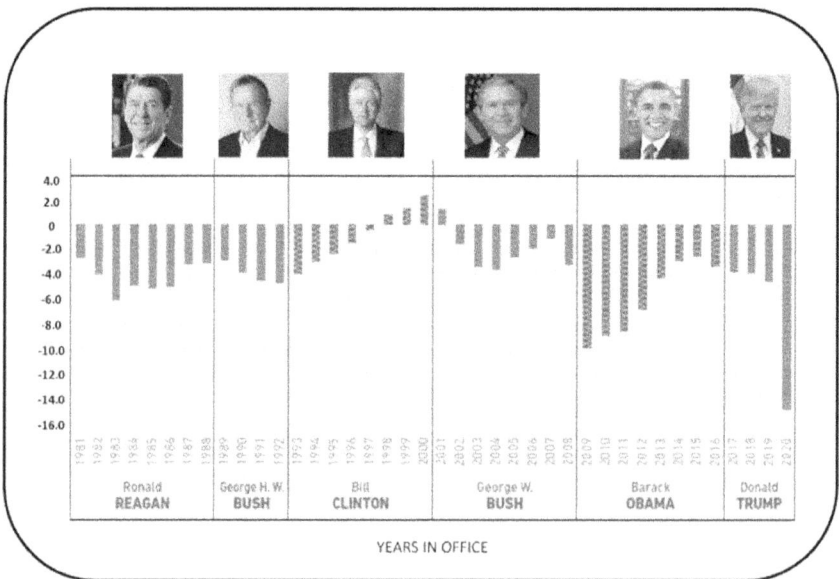

(This presidential spending chart was created by B. Whartnaby.)

Donald Trump increased the national debt by 40.43% - most of this in his last year in office, while Biden (in his first 2 years) has increased the debt by only 6.33%.[16]

Since President Putin has ruled Russia, its alarming economic growth has established it as a world leader. In 2000, their trade balance was plus $52 billion compared to the year 2018 when Russia's trade balance was a positive $165 billion[17]. In fact, by 2021 Russia had domination of the European gas and oil market, however since the Ukrainian War, Russia has lost a large percent of its European market. As of January 2023, "imports of Russian gas have fallen from 40% to 4% with some forecasts indicating Russia has lost the European gas market."[18]

Russia has been described by many as a soft power that orchestrates its political positions well.[19] Let me strongly state that Russian tactics are not due to any form of flaw, frailty, or softness.

"Putin's Chess Game," Artist – Jeff Koterba, Courtesy of Cagle Cartoons.

Washington Politicians who often ignore Russia's interests and its resources will be surprised to find themselves out maneuvered at every turn. As someone who gave up all my American comforts and my preconceived and fundamental beliefs that guided my judgement as an American in order to "become Russian," I can honestly tell you that many individuals in power positions in Washington, D.C. do not come close to understanding the cleverness of Putin or Russians. It would be better to think of Putin as a master chess player (not as good as Garry Kasparov of course) – constantly one step ahead. Because of Putin's basic Russian/KGB character, <u>he needs to feel as if he is in-control and winning</u> – and the only way to convince him to end the war in Ukraine would be to discover what would make Putin feel victorious – while Ukraine and the West accomplish their own separate goals. He probably needs to be offered a lucrative gas and oil deal and/or a promise from NATO. Gas and oil and other natural resources have made Putin a rich man, but since Europe is reducing dependence on Russian gas, this appears to be fluctuating and shifting.

No one, even Putin's closest aids, know his true reasoning behind the destruction of Ukraine. "Ukraine is one of four main pipeline corridors through which Russian gas flows to north, central, and southern Europe. In 2009, Russia accused Ukraine of diverting gas from Russian pipelines passing through Ukraine."[20] Is this the reason behind Putin's anger? I doubt it. As far back as 1997, Putin and his colleagues were discussing an invasion of Ukraine.

Who knows if Putin will ever comprehend that Europe may never work with Russia again due to his aggression and destruction of Ukrainian apartment homes, kindergartens, schools, hospitals, and other vital infrastructure and buildings – not to mention the number of lives lost? Putin's anger may even overflow into the use of nuclear weapons. If this happens, World War III would be imminent.

By January 2022, Russia amassed over 100,000 troops along the Ukrainian border.[21] The U.S., our allies, NATO, and everyone in Ukraine were concerned with a Russian invasion. Putin probably created this checkmate situation as a negotiating posture to get NATO to stop absorbing former Warsaw Pact countries into NATO - just a supposition. But remember, Putin is at his best when playing this form of military chess with the West – keeping the whole world off-balance while he decides which of his many options will best suite his long-term strategy.

Even worse, Putin's thoughts and plans may be more sinister. As far back as the mid to late 1990's, a 600+ page book surfaced that details Russian's strategic plans. This was during Putin's Vice President Days but during the period when Putin was expected to be the next President of Russia. He is presumed to be the "ghost" writer of this book called *The Foundations of Geopolitics*, which outlined Russia's plans for world dominance, and included are their steps to invade Ukraine. This book was published around 1997-1998 – twenty plus years ago. So the question is WHY has Putin decided to begin this invasion of Ukraine at this time? Is it because he believes that the United States is now sufficiently weakened – due to four years of Trump's mismanagement – that we cannot afford another war? Our country operates with a 28.1 trillion dollar debt ceiling (as of January 2022)[22] and with a large portion of this indebtedness to China. Has Russia and China reached an agreement, whereby China will not lend the U.S. additional funds? Or worse, will China call their debt due? We already owe them over one trillion dollars.[23] Is it because Trump (led by Putin) has created such a huge divide in our country that our government is no longer functioning? The Democrats and Republicans in Washington, D.C. no longer agree on what's best for the country and only fight over what is important for their respective parties – it's a "me-me" atmosphere in D.C. Is it because Putin now believes the U.S. and our democracy is ready to implode? This Russian invasion and war in Ukraine may be the final nail in the democracy coffin worldwide – not just in Ukraine, but also in the U.S., France, U.K., Finland, Poland, and a host of other democratic nations. The entire world is teetering on the brink of World War III – and what if WWIII meant the U.S., U.K., France, Poland, and Germany (and a few other smaller nations) against China and Russia who might be joined by Iran or others?

Furthermore, China has been flying their spy balloons over U.S. military bases and sites for at least the last 6 years.[24] It was also reported that three similar Chinese Spy balloons were hovering over the United States during the Trump era.[25]

The reason that China is flying these surveillance balloons over U.S. military sites should be obvious – they want to learn more about our military capabilities. Is this because they are preparing to invade Taiwan? Biden has already committed U.S. troops to protect the island of Taiwan – but at what cost to the American tax payer? Can we afford to fight a war in Ukraine AND a war in Taiwan?

In the past three to four decades, China has monopolized international trade. Just about everything in the U.S. that we consume comes from China. China has been among the world's fastest-growing economies since transforming and opening up their foreign trade and foreign investment(s). They implemented free-market reforms in 1979.[26] Their actual annual gross domestic product (GDP) growth averaged 9.5% through 2018, compared to the U.S. GDP through 2018 at 2.3%. This percentage gap continues to grow and impact the U.S. economy negatively.[27]

It has to be recognized that in 2020 both the Chinese and the Russians were among the world's top four economic leaders. China just celebrated its one-hundredth anniversary of governing as a communist country.[28] Russia's government has been "communist" since the 1920s except for a decade from 1991 to 2000 under Yeltsin.

Under Putin, the country operates with KGB/FSB men in every single discernible government position and is a closely controlled dictatorship. To provide an example, if you are the Minister of Agriculture – you work for the KGB/FSB. If you are Russian and you live in Australia but your family still lives in Russia, you work for the KGB/FSB if they need you because otherwise, your family will be threatened, imprisoned, or killed. Putin is the ONLY person in control. It is a God-Father type of mob, only 100,000,000 times worse and the tentacles of this mob reach out to every corner of the globe and even into space. And if you are Donald Trump and you had sex while in Russia, you can be sure there are photos of you in every position imaginable. Such photos are taken of every visiting foreigner possible and then stored until Putin needs them for bribery, persuasion, or inducement.

When Putin took office in 2000, the definition of Russian Government changed from a free-falling "socialist" state under Yeltsin, to a terrorizing dictatorship operated by a brotherhood of former KGB men. Once western businesses took hold in Moscow during the 1990s, materialism and western ideals began to flood major Russian cities. Russia returned to rule via a dictatorship but not the same type of communist regime as before Yeltsin. The gates of freedom opened first under Gorbachev and then more so under Yeltsin, and the populace embraced western-style products and goods. There were also certain freedoms, like travel outside of Russia, that were not available in the Soviet Union. Out of necessity, the Russian government had to adjust.

Russia has been ruthlessly governed under Putin, but conversely, he rebuilt his country from the chaos that he inherited from Yeltsin. Thinking as a Russian, I would be grateful to Putin for the modernized and economically strong Mother Land in the year 2020. Material goods are now available in grocery stores and GUMS (the largest Russian department store in Red Square), whereas before, the shelves were often empty. Before the war, the Russian Ruble more or less stabilized beginning in the mid-1990s when there were no credit or debit cards in the country. Public transportation and medical/dental care have improved. Russia's GDP continues to grow positively, so much so that Russia has established itself as among the top four economically stable countries worldwide –but again, this was before the war began. At no time during this process did Russian leaders – especially Putin – change their outlook on the United States. For Russian leaders, the Cold War never ended. Make no mistake, Putin envisions Russia successfully conquering other territories over time, as well as crippling or destroying his arch-enemy – the United States.

This is especially seen at the gas pumps and the grocery stores across the United States. When the price of a banana goes from $1.00 each to $3.50 or the price of one green pepper goes from 75 cents to $3.25 - it impacts every American household – and is due to Russia's cyber-attacks on our supply chains.

Our country, a democracy, is drastically indebted to China and Japan, primarily because we buy more products than we produce. In other words, our country operates in a deep dark fiscal hole. In the <u>Economist</u> March 2020,[29] the U.S. trade gap widened to $30.2 billion, and as of April 2020,[30] China held $1.07 trillion of our debt and Japan held $1.27 trillion of our debt.

"TRILLIONS SPENT FOR WHAT," ARTIST – MONTE WOLVERTON, COURTESY OF CAGLE CARTOONS

So, who really won the "cold war?" China, Russia, Japan, and Germany were among the world's economic powerhouse nations in 2020 during Trump's leadership. The United States was no longer on this list in 2021. President Biden has been rebuilding the U.S. economy and it is improving.

With our soaring debt to China and Japan, our enormous trade deficit, and Trump's alienation of other friendly nations, including NATO, the United States is no longer an economic leader of the free world. We can no longer afford to give away billions of dollars via USAID to build democracy in other countries. We cannot afford to support military bases in the Middle East or around the world. Our democracy is showing signs of collapse and/or insolvency. We need to rebuild our own economy by increasing manufacturing within the U.S. We cannot continue saving other countries and societies when our own country is economically so unstable.

The Moscow News, 23 January 2023 published an article called "Europe's Freedom Depends on Ukraine Winning a Decisive Victory Over Russia,"[31] written by Leonid Gozman. Mr. Gozman says:

"The international community seems to have understood that Ukraine must win this war, or at least that Putin cannot be allowed to emerge victorious. This understanding is fueled not so much by sympathy for Ukraine, but rather by the realization that Putin's regime is a threat to the whole of Western civilization. If Putin attains his goal of destroying Ukraine he will not be satisfied but will continue 'reclaiming what's his.' That is, the world has understood that no amount of appeasement will ever make peaceful coexistence with Vladimir Putin possible."

As of 2022, the United States has committed to investing $54 Billion[32] for the war in Ukraine. This assistance is broken down into: (1) Economic Support Fund $9.4 Billion, (2) Military and Security Assistance $6 Billion, (3) Weapons and Other Supplies $12.5 Billion, (4) Grants and Loans for Military Supplies $4.7 Billion, (5) Food assistance, health care, and other aid $7 Billion, (6) Migration and Refugee assistance $1.8 Billion, (7) Assistance for Europe, Eurasia, and Central Asia $1.1 Billion, (8) U.S. military deployments and intelligence $8.1 Billion, and (9) Other foreign aid $1.5 Billion.[33] While this investment is critically important to preserve the country of Ukraine, to save democracy worldwide, and to defeat President Putin's aggression - how can the United States afford to spend $54 Billion when our country's is operating in a hole? "Of the $54 Billion in total spending by the United States, $31.4 Billion can be considered transitional foreign aid... it is roughly two times the amount given in 2011 to Afghanistan, the largest U.S. foreign aid recipient until now... The U.S. has committed around three times as much money as all European Union countries combined..."[34]

This U.S. negative economic disaster grows exponentially annually and is reflected by the debt ceiling and the high interest rate we pay to borrow money from abroad. When Trump was in the White House, the debt ceiling was raised three times in four years.[35] How many times has the news reported to American citizens that our government is about to shut down? If the government shuts down, our country defaults on our debts including repayments to China and Japan. Would you continue to loan money, trillions of dollars, to someone who could not repay the loan? What happens to the funds allocated for Ukraine if our government shuts down?

In the 1960s and 1970s and beyond, large U.S. manufacturers outsourced their production to "third world" countries. This move drastically reduced the number of jobs available for blue-collar workers or those individuals who were under-educated in the United States. Of course modern technology was also a major influence on the U.S. job market, but those without a college education – namely because of the costs associated with college - found themselves constantly unemployed. Without income and jobs, many of these individuals resorted to dealing in drugs so that they could feed their families and pay their bills. Of course many individuals dealt in drugs because it was fast and easy money. The use of illegal drugs soared across our country and contributed to my decision to move to Russia. I did not want my children exposed to the epidemic of mind altering drugs found in U.S. schools.

This decision backfired because at that time "everyone" in Russia smoked – and there was no social marketing campaign teaching people the health risks of smoking. All four of my children smoked at one stage or another, but they have now managed to kick this habit.

As more and more of these individuals – primarily Black men – went to prison on drug charges, the dynamics of Black families changed from two parents to mothers only. And more often than not, these mothers needed welfare to care for their children – which resulted in the growth of the federal government and our society becoming a welfare state. This needs to be reversed for this country to economically prosper.

If we really want to change America, legislation needs to be created to require manufacturers or importers to produce a large percentage of their products in the U.S., because despite our economic woes, the U.S. is still the target market for goods. This will result in more jobs and perhaps less incarceration of Black men. Black men are the majority population in prisons across the U.S. and our country has incarcerated in excess of two million individuals – more than any nation worldwide.[36]

Our national prison system has become just another capitalist scheme – the occupancy of prison beds directly relates to its revenue and profits – more prisoners means more money. And while the rate of prisoner release has increased, so has the number of ex-cons who return to prison due to parole violations. The Department of Corrections more often than not also controls parole. This statistic is under-reported and distorted. It is a revolving door approach to justify the Department of Corrections budget and is a broken system that perhaps should be a focus for reorganization and cutting massive costs.

Taxing the wealthy, those who earn more than $400,000 annually, is not a substitute for the government tightening its own belt by reducing expenditures. Taxing large corporations might be a source of federal revenue, however we need to keep these businesses in the United States and not alienate them by taxing profits beyond reason. To create sustainable employment, these jobs should be government-funded initially (no interest loans since this money was initially paid by taxpayers) for private businesses, but only for a limited period of time. Each business must create and follow an approved business plan, and be accountable for the actionable steps that demonstrate financial growth, sustainability, and stability.

This concept is nearly the same principal used to operate micro-credit programs, only on a larger scale. Both in Russia and in Central Asia, I was the senior manager for six micro-credit programs. In fact, five of these programs transitioned into a micro-finance organization, which is similar to a credit union in the United States. [13] We had to work with local and federal Kazakh government authorities and an old-world communist banking system in order to establish new laws and to create a new type of banking entity. Called Asia Credit, its portfolio has grown into a multi-million dollar organization in Central Asia. Credit needs to go to Mercy Corps International and the many Kazakh and American employees who perfected this specific enterprise model so that it achieved not only operational self-sufficiency but also financial self-sufficiency which results in sustainability.

And every year, as the U.S. goes further into debt, Russia becomes more and more powerful. Putin, plans long-term, sees the bigger picture, knows his next strategic move, and is constantly watching the U.S. and is entertained. However, it appears that Putin failed to fully envision the world's reaction to his invasion of Ukraine.

I love the U.S. but our form of democracy is in serious trouble. Our economy is in a negative and plummeting free-fall, our democratic government is not working for the benefit of all of our citizens, federal troops have invaded American cities, and we lead the world in the spread of the pandemic. In addition, every year, we see an increase in costly natural disasters from coast to coast, such as catastrophic hurricanes, tornados, floods, and unstoppable, raging forest fires. Such disasters annually cost our federal government billions of dollars. There is no indication that these disasters will subside, in fact they appear to worsen annually.

Fortunately, by 2021 the chant of "wear masks and practice safe distancing" has helped control the COVID-19 virus. Vaccines are being administered at a fast rate under new presidential leadership to ensure protection for our citizens. Yet, there are many Trump supporters who continue to believe his conspiracy theories and refuse to accept the COVID vaccine protection. Our country will never eradicate COVID-19 unless more people are vaccinated. Just like the vaccines for the polio epidemic of the 1950s and the smallpox virus (which was eradicated in the 1980s), the COVID-19 vaccine is the only realistic and proven solution to protect our society, our schools, our workplaces and our families.

"Vaccine Hesitancy 2", Artist – Dave Whamond, Courtesy of Cagle Cartoons.

The American Rescue Plan[37], implemented by President Biden, will cost the U.S. approximately $1.9 trillion. The Infrastructure Plan[38] is estimated to be $2.5 trillion. While I believe both of these plans are essential to rebuild our economy, save millions of small businesses, rebuild roads and bridges, pay for education, and put Americans back to work – I am worried about the price tag and our national debt.

Keep in mind that it was only in 2019 when former President Trump spent twice as much as the U.S. Treasury raised in taxes and other sources of revenue. This deficit must be considered before our Congress approves trillions of dollars for other causes or gives billions of dollars to other countries. How is this Trump debt going to be repaid?

Meanwhile, the police across our country continue to kill Black men, women, and children. In the case of George Floyd, the evidence was obvious and televised. The repeated offenses are so chronic and systemic that it may be past time for corrective action but we must not give up hope. Festering racial hatred has hurt the United States. It is cruel and inhumane, YET it reflects our society and all of those who live here. Each of us is complicit if we do nothing to change this injustice. Our government is willing to spend $54 Billion to save Ukraine and Billions more to build roads and bridges – but if we do not make a large investment in resolving our racism, violence, mass shootings, hatred, and police brutality then OUR DEMOCRACY may not survive.

The national debt as of the end of 2021 was $31.46 trillion dollars.[39] "This debt is defined as the amount of money the federal government has borrowed to cover the outstanding balance of expenses incurred over time. Simply put, the national debt is similar to a person using a credit card for purchases and not paying off the full balance each month. The cost of purchases exceeding the amount paid off represents a deficit, while accumulated deficits over time represents a person's overall debt."[40]

"Racism is a leading cause of death in the United States."[41] In addition, there is a cost[42] associated with our racism and Dana Peterson[43] estimates that this cost is approximately $8 Trillion dollars per decade. This cost does not include the large settlements achieved in court by the families of those Black men who have been killed.

By exploiting hatred and racism in the U.S. we are drastically increasing our debt. Americans need to understand that Putin has used any method possible to destroy our country and that includes any scheme to increase our national debt. The Ukraine war has cost the United States so far $54 Billion allocated over ten years – a decade. Hatred, racism, mass murders, and violence all cost the government money and these funds come out of taxpayer pockets

I doubt that Donald Trump even understands that his buddy – Vladimir Putin – is guiding him to destroy our country, but this exactly what has happened from 2015 to 2021.

It is our responsibility to protect our citizens for the privilege of living in a democracy.

Trump seriously damaged America and is continuing to play his silly and deceitful games even after leaving the White House. Rather than uniting our citizens and our country under one flag, we are more fractured than at any time in the history of this nation except for the civil war. Trump's televised comments and speeches were full of hatred, bigotry, and pointing the finger of blame at others for his own mistakes instead of accepting responsibility. This hatred and bigotry have been passed from Trump to the police and others who then enact this abhorrence and horror. More importantly, media across the U.S. has daily broadcasted Trump and his lies – therefore unknowingly spreading this disinformation.

"Tired of Winning?," Artist – Bruce Plante, Courtesy of Cagle Cartoons.

People – especially the U.S. Republican voting public – seem to believe that their elected Senators did not vote to impeach Trump because it was the right thing to do or that January sixth was acceptable – both are wrong assumptions. Let me repeat; those embarrassing elected officials did not vote against Trump because of their FEAR of his reprisal or revenge. There were only ten Republican Senators who were brave enough to impeach Trump. Due to Trump's bullying and dictator-like behavior – and the behavior of his followers, they immediately begun harassing those ten Senators and threatening the lives of their children. htt ps://www.businessinsider.com. "Representative Swalwell got a voicemail threatening to 'cut off his kids heads' . . . " August 14, 2022.

Are we on the verge of another American civil war? Are there viable solutions, or are we to continue this tumbling spiral into a moral abyss – where the men and women hired to protect our communities are actually killing our innocent citizens? Do we want to live in a country controlled by one man, or do we want our democracy to work? Is this how we want our tax dollars spent and the country we want our children to inherit, or is blind loyalty to a political party or one man more important to us?

Blind loyalty to a political party or leader is how Hitler conquered Germany and claimed the minds of an entire nation[44] where good people were transformed into brutal mass killers, filled with ethnic hatred that led to the death of about six million human beings.[45] We – the United States with people believing and following Trump's lies - are on our way to mimic that same gruesome and murderous historical episode as Nazi Germany. In 2020, violence has increased in our country by 30%.[46]

"Our Unstable Democracy", Artist – Dave Whamond, Courtesy of Cagle Cartoons.

Many people in the U.S. believed Trump concerning COVID. Some of these people have died. Others believed that it was an assault on their personal rights and freedoms to be mandated to wear a mask. These same individuals are the ones now spreading this disease (in Republican states such as Florida, Texas, Arizona, Alabama, Alaska, and others)[47] and are the same individuals who do not seem to understand that if Trump had been allowed to continue his destruction of the U.S. government, our economy, and our democracy, that all personal rights and freedoms could have been abolished – the least of which would be refusing to wear a mask.

The detestation generated by the Trump administration permeated every home in America. He has systematically transformed our democracy – our first amendment rights to free speech and the right to assemble – into a federally-controlled domestic military war zone. Like Putin in his first few years in power in Russia, Trump squelched anyone who opposes him and continues this detestable action. And, just like the uncontrolled virus indiscriminately ravaging the bodies of millions of Americans (over forty-two million as of the end of 2020)[48] Trump infected our nation with a mantra of hatred, racism, and dishonest conspiracy stories to consume the thoughts and minds of those who are willing to believe him. The process that put him in power could so easily consume this country and defeat our version of democracy and freedom.

For example, this author was at a Tucson, AZ. Barnes and Noble for a book signing event. One middle-aged woman came up to me and said "I believe Putin is a wonderful leader."[49] These are the exact same words spoken by Trump several times especially in support of the Russian invasion of Ukraine.[50]

At the end of May 2021, 70% of the Republicans in the U.S. still believed that Trump won the 2020 presidential election.[51] This lie is political propaganda and was instigated by Trump himself on live national TV.[52] Yet, some people irrationally have confidence in every word out of Trump's mouth. This is not only difficult to comprehend, but is a sign of "mob mentality" whereby people have been brain-washed – a method to thoroughly alter beliefs or ways of thinking.

Brain-washing initiated in totalitarian countries, was used universally in Germany by Hitler, and was absorbed by Putin during his tenure there as a masterful way to sway minds and distort reality when dealing with large populations. It has now been used in the United States.

What is Hatred and How is it Related to Brainwashing?[53]

"*Brainwashing is the concept that the human mind can be altered or controlled by certain psychological techniques. Brainwashing is said to reduce its subject's ability to think critically . . . to allow the introduction of new and unwanted thoughts and to change attitudes, values, and beliefs. The term 'brainwashing' was first used in English by Edward Hunter in 1950 to describe how the Chinese government appeared to make people cooperate with them. Research into this concept also looked at Nazi Germany and the actions of human traffickers . . . and in the conversion of people to groups which (often) are considered to be cults.*[54]

"*Russian historian Daniel Romanovsky, who interviewed survivors and eyewitnesses in the 1970s, reported on what he called 'Nazi brainwashing' of the people of Belarus by the occupying Germans during the Second World War, which took place through both mass propaganda (repeated lies) and intense re-education . . . Romanovsky noted that very soon most people had adopted the Nazi view that the Jews were an inferior race . . .*"[55]

Hatred is a very angry emotional response towards ideas or certain people. . . and is often associated with intense feelings of anger and contempt. Hatred changes the chemistry in the brain. It stimulates the area in the brain responsible for planning and execution of motion, and this part triggers aggression while feeling hateful to either defend or attack."[56]

The SPLC (Southern Poverty Law Center) published an article on Facebook and Twitter called "*Tell (former) President Trump to Take Responsibility for the Hate He's Unleased.*"[57] This article states:

"*President Trump's campaign and presidency have energized the white supremacist movement in unprecedented ways. We saw it in the support he received from David Duke (an American white supremacist anti-Semitic conspiracy theorist, convicted felon, and former Grand Wizard of the KKK) in his campaign. We saw it in the surge in hate crimes committed in his name after the election. And we saw it in the deadly gathering of white supremacists in Charlottesville."[58]*

Trump's hate-filled speeches, tweets, and mass propaganda were forms of brain-washing which unleased vile hatred toward any person Trump mentioned or alluded to, like when Pence would not break the law and do as Trump wanted during the Senate election certification process on January 6, 2021.

This hatred continues with a social cost. USA Today[59], published an article by Candy Woodall, July 8, 2022, and it states the following:

"A number of GOP candidates have spent hundreds of millions of dollars on ads this campaign season pushing "replacement theories and other conspiracies targeting people of color while also attacking fellow Republicans who don't fall in line. During the 2022 midterm cycle, more than 2,700 ads have aired on television and social media focusing on racist tropes. Without a doubt, there are serious downstream consequences.

A Buffalo, New York gunman who has been charged with a hate crime for the mass shooting of 10 Black shoppers at a Buffalo supermarket. He referenced the racist replacement theory 10 times in his writings before the shooting. The gunman said Black people were "replacers" of white Americans."[60]

This increase in ethnic hate crimes was partially due to the hateful Trump speeches given to the U.S. public. After four years of listening to Trump, a large proportion of U.S. citizens were so brainwashed that they believed anything mentioned by Trump.[62]

> **Hatred is a tool used in brainwashing to convince individuals and groups to act out violent crimes. There is a really clear relationship between political hateful speeches and mass murder or other criminal activities."**
> (USA Today, Cindy Woodall, July 8th 2022)

I am pleading with you – every citizen of the United States – to view 2016 to 2021 as a major national digression plummeting our democratic nation into a chaotic land filled with one lie after another, with blind hatred, and with lethal violence. This hatred and these lies have turned us against our neighbors, co-workers, and even family. They also have convinced groups of unassuming people that they are working toward saving our country, when in reality they are destroying it through all negative actions and thoughts such as: hatred, lying, violence, and racism.

By dividing our nation into red or blue, we are a weakened nation –which is exactly what Putin wanted and planned! Our entire nation has been manipulated by a Russian chess master and he continues to do so on a daily basis. Every time you hear about Russian cyber security threats or ransomware, remember that Putin is behind these destructive raids on the United States infrastructure. So far his cyber-attacks include our massive and essential gas and oil business, our banking networks, our gridiron of food and supply distributions, and even more importantly on several vital departments of the U.S. Government.

"Russia's Cyber Attack on U.S. Meat", Artist – Dave Granlund, Courtesy of Cagle Cartoons.

"The West and especially the United States naively believed that the West had won the Cold War. This was a momentous and critical mistake. When Bush Senior said the Cold War is over and a new era of cooperation is beginning, that was it. But the Russians used cooperation to deceive the U.S. . . . Americans are like children and think, 'If you are cooperating, you're cooperating. . . No questions asked – even if the Russians are holding a brick behind their backs. The door had been left open for the Russians to funnel black cash into the U.S. And according to Shvets in Putin's People, the Russians needed to find more "subtle ways to launder cash through businesses and not directly through U.S. banks. And there was Trump and his financial problems."63

For the Russians, Trump was the KGB textbook resolution. But to listen to Trump say "he has no ties to Russia or to Russians" is beyond fabrication.64 This book attempts to explain to all U.S. citizens about the Russian threat to the U.S. The impact of Russia's interference in our economy is so much greater than the average American realizes including our government leaders. It is time for all Americans to WAKE UP.

Here is an example. In spring 2022, the U.S. was faced with an enormous shortage of infant and baby formula.65 There was a whole list of reasons provided to the American consumers for this shortage. The number one reason was due to a product recall, but also due to the Pandemic. Since Russians have hacked into so many of our essential product supply chains, my first reaction was to look at Russia. The following is the published statement made by Cargill, a large U.S. agricultural company operating in Russia since the mid 1990's regarding their potential pull-out from Russia. (Due to the Ukrainian War).

"Note: This region (Russia) plays a significant role in our global food system and is a critical source of key ingredients in basic staples like bread, infant formula, and cereal."66

I am not the least surprised by this statement and I also realize this U.S. shortage had no connection with the American management of Cargill in Russia. However, once product(s) leaves the company's oversight, only Putin and his "thugs" have control over the delivery schedules and supply and demand of products and their destinations. My guess is that somewhere along the supply chain for baby formula, there is a forced delay caused by Russian hackers. It would be naïve to believe otherwise, especially considering the massive U.S. military assistance to Ukraine which has infuriated Putin to the point of threatening nuclear war.

So who really won the Cold War?

CHAPTER 2 – END NOTES

1 https://www.history.com/topics/world-war-ii. "The Bombing of Hiroshima and Nagasaki on August 6, 1945." Updated on July 25, 2022 from the original on November 18, 2009. This article states: "On August 6, 1945, during World War II (1939-1945), an American B-29 bomber dropped the world's first deployed atomic bomb over the Japanese city of Hiroshima. The explosion immediately killed an estimated 80,000 people; tens of thousands more would later die of radiation exposure. Three days later, a second B-29 dropped another A-bomb on Nagasaki, killing an estimated 40,000 people."

2https://bea.gov/news/blog/2018-trade-gap (BEA is the Bureau of Economic Analysis).

3 Ibid.

4 Ibid.

5 https:www.bis.doc.gov, "U.S. Trade with China in 2020.

6 https://wits.worldbank.org, "Russia Trade Summary 2018."

7 https://www.cbo.gov, "The Federal Budget in Fiscal Year 2020."

8 *Putin's People*, written by Catherine Belton.

9 Ibid, p. 453.

10 Ibid.

11 Ibid.

12 Ibid, p.457.

13 https://www.usatoday.com/mews/world/2017/01/11. "Trump says "I have nothing to do with Russia" 'That's not exactly true.", USA Today, written by Jessica Durando, January 11, 2017.

14 https://abcnews.go.com, July 2016 updated by Brian Ross and Matthew Mosk on Jan. 30, 2017. "US-Russian Businessman Said to be Source of Key Trump Dossier Claims." Sergei Millian was the President of the Russian-American Chamber of Commerce.

15 https://www.thebalancemoney.com/trade-policy.

16 What's the National Debt by President?, Written by Beth Luthi, September 26, 2022.

17 https://www.macrotrends.net/russia "Russia's trade balance for 2018 was $165.83B, a 98.56% increase from 2017.

18 https://www.accenture.com/us-en/insights/energy. "The Impact of War in Ukrraine on Oil & Gas Industry." May 10, 2022, written by Muqsit Ashraf, Vivek Chidambaram, and a host of others.

19 https://eng.globalaffairs.ru/articles. "The Rise and Fall of Russia's Soft Power." Written by VD Ageeva.

20 https://www.politico.eu/article/russian-gas-across-uk. Written by America Hernandez, September 28, 2022.

21 https://www.nytimes.com, "Pentagon: Russia Has More Than 100,000 Troops at Ukraine's Border." January 28, 2022.

22 https://www.nytimes.com/U.S./Politics, "America Hit its Debt Limit, Setting up Bitter Fiscal Fight," written by Jim Tankersley and Alan Rappeport. January 2022.

23 The Economy, "How Large Is the U.S. Debt to China?" written by David Moadel, September 5, 2022.

24 https://www.cnn.com. "China Spy Balloon: Everything you need to know." February 4, 2023.

25 Ibid.

26 https://everycrsreport.com "China's Economic Rise: History Trends, Challenges, and Implications for the United States, July 12, 2006 to June 25, 2019." "Since opening up to foreign trade and investment and implementing free-market reforms in 1979, China has been among the world's fastest growing economies, with real annual gross domestic product growth averaging 9.5% through 2018, a pace described by the World Bank as "the fastest sustained expansion by a major economy in history."

27 Ibid.

28 https://en.wikipedia.org/wiki/100th_Anniverserity_of_the_Chinese-Communist-Party.

29 The Economist, March 2020 and April 2020.

30 Ibid.

31 The Moscow News, 23 January 2023. "Europe's Freedom Depends on Ukraine Winning a Decisive Victory Over Russia," Written by Leonid Gozman.

32 The New York Times, "Four Ways to Understand the $54 Billion in U.S. Spending on Ukraine," Written by Biance Pallaro and Alicia Parlapiano, May 20, 2022.

33 Ibid.

34 Ibid.

35 https://www.indems.org/fact-check. "The national debt has risen by almost $7.8 trillion during Trump's time in office. INGOP raised the debt limit three times.."

36 https://wwwsentencingproject.org/research. There are 2 million people in the nation's prisons and jails – a 500% increase over the last 40 years." September 8, 2022.

37 https://www.congress.gov-bill. H.R. 1319 – 117th Congress created to provide emergency grants, lending, and investment to hard-hit small businesses.

38 https://whitehouse.gov. The bipartisan Infrastructure Investment Plan and Jobs Act will invest about $110 billion for roads, bridges, and major projects such as ensuring that every American has access to reliable high-speed internet.

39 https://fiscaldata.treasury.gov. "Understanding the National Debt."

40 Ibid.

41 https://medicareadvocacy.org. Study: Racism is a Leading Cause of Death in the United States." This article states: "Black people in the United States are more likely to die young – not because there is some intrinsic biological risk, but because of racism." January 27, 2022.

42 https://www.youtube.com. "The High Cost of Racism," by Dana Peterson. "She came up with an estimate of $16 trillion dollars over two decades." March 21, 2022.

43 https://www.linkedin.com. Dana Peterson is a Global Economist with Citi Research, New York, N.Y.

44 https://www.slate.com. "How Hitler Conquered Germany." The Nazi propaganda machine exploited ordinary Germans by encouraging them to be co-producers of a false reality."

45 https://www.pnas.org. "Nazi indoctrination and anti-Semitic believes in Germany." "Significance Attempts at modifying public opinions, attitudes, and beliefs range from advertising and schooling to brainwashing."

46 https://pewresearch.org. "What we know about the increase in U.S. murders in 2020. The U.S. murder rate rose 30% between 2019 and 2020 – the largest single-year increase in more than a century. Pew Research Center, October 27, 2021."

47 https://globalhealth.harvard.edu. "Cases and Deaths Are Surging in Southern States," July 16, 2020.

48 "COVID-19 Infected Many More Americans in 2020 than Official Tallies Show" Published in *Nature*, September 7, 2021, Written by Dr. Francis Collins."

49 https://www.quora.com. "Why does Trump think that Putin is a good leader . . ." April 30, 2017.

50 https://abcnews.go.com. "As Putin eyes Ukraine invasion, Trump praises his actions as 'genius'. Written by Olivia Rubin, February 23, 2022."

51 https://www.pounter.org, Fact Checking. "Most Republicans still falsely believe Trump's stolen election claims. About 70 of Republicans say they don't think Joe Biden is the legitimate winner of the 2020 election."

52 https:www.abcnews.go.com "Trump has a longstanding history of calling elections 'rigged' if he doesn't like the results." Written by Terrance Smith., November 11, 2020.

53 Google, January 27, 2021. "How Hatred Affects the Brain."

54 Ibid.

55 Ibid.

56 *Google, Jan. 27, 2021, "How Hatred Affects the Brain."*

57 The Southern Poverty Law Center, "Tell (former) President Trump to Take Responsibility for the Hate He's Unleashed."

58 Ibid.

59 https://usatoday.com/Candy-Woodall, article on Trump and hatred, July 8, 2022.

60 Ibid.

61 The FBI Statistical Crime Data Base.

62 USA Today, Cindy Woodall, July 8, 2022.

63 Putin's People, Catherine Belton, page 459.

64 https://www.usatoday.com. "Trump says he has 'nothing to do with Russia – no deals, no loans, no nothing." January 11, 2017, written by Jessica Durando.

65 https://www.cnbc.com, "What you need to know about the U.S. baby formula shortage,"

66 *www.cargill.com/Cargill's Statement Regarding Their Russian Operations.*

Chapter Three

Police And The Military

O ur crime statistics show that U.S. society's brutality and violence continues to grow exponentially with each generation of Americans. Power and control have replaced the intrinsic and self-controlling moral value system that informally governed Americans forty to sixty years ago and appears to be the basis for much of the violence that occurs today. The good ole "right vs. wrong" has transitioned into shades of gray. This is true in domestic violence, assault cases, and homicides. Laws are on the books, but these same laws can be distorted and manipulated to protect the rich and powerful more than the average American Black man who cannot afford the best attorney or the largest law firm.

There have been many studies that show the U.S. leads the developed world in violence and crime.[1] In fact, there is no other developed country that compares. In September 2021, Kiara Aflonsecxa of ABC News reported that "A New Study highlights a pattern of racism in policing and more than half of U.S. killings by police go unreported."[2]

Russia was the opposite of this during the communist reign. During the early 1990s and before, you could walk your dog on any street in any major Russian city at any time, day or night, and know that you were safe. In St. Petersburg, it is still daylight at midnight during the summer months and the sky is magnificent. I often walked my dogs late at night when I lived there. Petty theft was not tolerated by any city in Russia, and prison terms were stiff. Prisons in Russia are not like the luxurious prisons found in the U.S., with clean clothes and food served daily. Russian prisons were cold, dirty, and ruthless, with little to no food. Often the only food for a prisoner came from his immediate family. If a person was sent to prison in Russia, even if the crime was murder, they could be released if a member of their family paid the "ransom" or if their family knew someone who held a high political office.

The U.S. society is living with the long-term after-effects of decades of warfare and armed conflict. Our men, and an increasing number of women, have been coming home from war almost every decade since WWII – Korea, Viet Nam, the Mid-East and Gulf Wars, the Afghanistan War, and the Iraq War.[3]

Once home and out of the military, these same men and women often join their local police departments. They are good candidates and trained in the use of firearms. They use the same military war tactics taught by our government in performing police work. This means excessive violence that often results in the deaths of the very people they are hired to protect. Not only that, but too many have the attitude that it is "them against the bad guy – the enemy." Sadly, in domestic situations, the bad guys are too often the innocent dark-skinned boy or man walking home with a bag of groceries.

"The Talk", Artist – John Darkow, Courtesy of Cagle Cartoons.

It appears that the increased levels of police violence in our country may be directly proportional to the number of veterans reenacting the violence of war on the home front once they become police officers.

The Trump administration purportedly and mistakenly claimed that militarizing the police reduces crime. The Federal 1033 program[4] provides military surplus equipment to domestic police departments, but there is little accurate data to suggest a correlation with a reduction in local crime. However, the obvious fact, contrary to what Trump said, is that the U.S. military (men, women, and equipment) is designed to fight wars abroad to protect our country, while the local police departments are intended to protect local citizens on local streets. He confused the role of the military and actually ordered federal troops into American cities. More specifically, his choice of cities was based on which cities in the U.S. have elected Democrat mayors or Black mayors. This has increased the level of violence, alienated local residents, and was clearly a political, dictator-type of decision.

Jeff Sessions, an attorney general under Trump, relied on findings from studies published in the American Economic Journal to say that "military aid reduces street-level" crime and that the "display of military equipment" causes criminals to rethink committing crimes.[5] Both are totally wrong assumptions.

These misleading conclusions were based on evidence from the 1033 Program, which allows the Defense Logistics Agency to send police departments various military weapons and equipment. 1033 has been described as "Uncle Sam's Goodwill Store." Local and state police departments can request military surplus (of unknown quality) as it becomes available — including items as varied as assault rifles, armored vehicles, computers, and tube socks. All they have to pay for is shipping. Data on the program shows a long list of shipments from the federal government to local and state police.

Studies on this program used standard techniques to counter possible biases.[6] However, the data was incomplete. The data recorded what agencies had on hand in 2014 but did not accurately report when they received it or what they had before. Weapons and gear can be returned, destroyed, or obtained from other local police departments or state coordinators — but the data did not record any of that vital information. The researchers couldn't know what police had in the past, so any conclusions they drew were based on an inaccurate history.

*" Oops, I meant to grab the **car**. "*

"Police Error," Artist – Peter Kuper, Courtesy of Cagle Cartoons.

The obvious and common-sense conclusion of the 1033 Program that transfers military equipment to local police is that this equipment was originally created for our military to use abroad against our enemies in war-like settings. Local police departments are intended to protect local citizens and arrest local criminals – not kill them.

Local police are NOT the judge or the jury.

Additionally, studies have shown that those police officers with military experience are more prone to commit local shootings and killings and to use unnecessary force and brutality.[7]

Men and women who have been trained to kill in the U.S. military should not transition into local police officers, or before they do, there should be a law required to readjust their mindset and their violent trained instinct to kill.

U.S. citizens of any race, color, or gender should not be a "target" of local police – who need to grasp that they are employed to "protect" their communities and all the residents.

The George Floyd Justice in Policing Act of 2021 passed the House of Representatives on March 3, 2021.[8] It stalled in the Senate due to bipartisan squabbling and was still not approved by September 2021. The most important issue in Bill H.R. 1280 is law enforcement accountability and policing practices, but it also addresses law enforcement misconduct. Just as important, it outlines training requirements and launches policing best practices. The shoulders of Senator Cory Booker has been burdened with the task of passing this Bill, but this weight is far too cumbersome for his shoulders alone. He needs all of us across the U.S. to support him in this effort.

Passing of this Bill is an important step toward reducing the number of police murders of innocent Blacks in our country, but it is not the all-encompassing answer. It is the mindset of our society that must change – especially our White population - from hatred to acceptance of others.

Just imagine that you are living in a typical middle-class White suburban area. A new young White family moves in. There is a mother, father, and one child who is six years old. The boy socially meets with other families of young children in the neighborhood. The children play together and go to school on the same bus. After a year, the new child's skin begins to become darker and darker, and by his seventh birthday he looks African-American. Neighbors stop socializing with this new family and he is shunned at school. The family is no longer invited to other neighborhood activities. It turns out this child has a rare, skin pigmentation disease and there is no cure. However, this condition is contagious. Other children in the neighborhood begin to show signs of their skin becoming darker. What do you think would happen in this U.S. neighborhood? "We live in a country and a society which is grounded on "all men are created equal." BUT ARE WE?

This change should begin with our leadership – a top-down approach through a nationwide social marketing campaign, and from the bottom-up with each of us working toward the goal of equality, forgiveness, and respect for others.

In the December 1997, <u>Life Magazine</u>, author and lecturer Marianne Williamson[9] wrote:

"The dominant 20th century Western world has sucked the spiritual life force out of us. We have experienced tremendous material and technological progress, but as a civilization we are spiritually bereft. Gandi said we must choose between "soul force" and "brute force." That defines the crossroads of the world right now. We have two choices: to become soulful and soul-filled people, or on some level "to become brutes." In the last thirty years especially, we have put money before the soul. That's got to change."

There is no better explanation to interpret why I choose to live in Russia, although at the time I made that decision such exemplary reasoning was not within my grasp of understanding. Anyone who has spent time in Russia has heard the term "the Russian soul." This book is partially about that transition – from the western world's dream of materialism and wealth to the Russian world's depth of soul – and all the misunderstandings, the pain, the naiveté, the ineptitude, the struggles, and yes, the western arrogance that accompanied this transference.

This process was tough, but it has been even tougher to watch Trump destroy my homeland by his speeches full of hatred and lies repeated ceaselessly. It sent chills up my spine, since this type of leadership was a reflection of and a duplication of what I had experienced in Russia and other countries lead by ruthless dictators. Even worse, people believed his lies, people repeated them, and our media daily propagated these lies by making Trump a daily news headline.

People who are/were totally brainwashed by Trump and his repetition of lies – believe Trump no matter what he says. It doesn't matter if he is seen on NBC, MSNBC, ABC, or FOX – the more he is seen on TV and the more his lies are heard – THE MORE HE WILL BE BELIEVED. The secret to detoxify Trump's cult followers is to stop broadcasting his hurtful lies or anything about him. DO NOT SHOW TRUMP ON TV.

CHAPTER 3 – END NOTES

1 https://everytownresearch.org "Gun Violence in America, updated January 26, 2022."

2 ABC News, "A New Study highlights a pattern of racism in policing and more than half of U.S. killings by police go unreported.", Written by Kiara Aflonsecxa, September 2021.

3 https://en.wikipedia.org. "List of Wars involving the United States."

4 https://www.dia.mil/, The 1033 Program operated by the Defense Logistics Agency.

5 https://vocativ.com. In Jeff Sessions's America, A Tank for Every Cop. May 24, 2017. Written by James King.

6 https://www/aclu, "Federal Militarization of Law Enforcement must End, May 12, 2021."

7 Ibid.

8 https://www.congress.gov_bill. H.R. 1280 – 117th Congress (2021-2022). "This bill establishes a framework to prevent and remedy racial profiling by law enforcement at the federal, state, and local levels."

9 Life Magazine, Author and lecturer Marianne Williamson, December 1997.

Chapter Four

The People Have Spoken

A cross the nation and around the world, tens of thousands of demonstrators have voiced their outrage at the George Floyd murder at the hands of a Milwaukee policeman.[1] The message was loud and clear, that police brutality in the U.S. has to stop. It can no longer be denied – not just by the Black communities but by all of humanity. Murder is murder. Abuse of power is abuse of power, and hatred leads to violence.

> **If you value human life, then realize this pattern of hatred and violence must stop.**

IF YOU SUCCUMB TO THE TEMPTATION OF USING VIOLENCE IN YOUR STRUGGLE UNBORN GENERATIONS WILL BE THE RECIPIENTS OF A LONG AND DESOLATE NIGHT OF BITTERNESS AND YOUR CHIEF LEGACY WILL BE AN ENDLESS REIGN OF MEANINGLESS CHAOS.

THE ARIZONA DAILY STAR 2021

"MLK Jr. Wisdom for the Right," Artist – David Fitzsimmons, Courtesy of Cagle Cartoons

Through TV broadcasts and social media, video clips proliferated the violence as everyone saw police officers detaining and cuffing an on-duty deliveryman, in spite of the protection his "essential worker" status supposedly affords; and police officers tear-gassing an unassuming and innocent captive crowd in a park. In October 2021, a police officer pulled a paraplegic Black man out of his car by his hair.[2]

Two Buffalo police officers were suspended without pay after being caught on video knocking down an elderly White man during a peaceful demonstration and leaving him in a pool of blood. This graphic video went viral June 4, 2020 and prompted widespread outrage. In the video, the protester, who was seventy-five-years old, was seen approaching a line of police in Buffalo's Niagara Square and appeared to be trying to talk to the officers, who were dressed in riot gear. The police then knocked him down and left him bleeding on the pavement. [3] This video was shown endlessly on live TV across our nation, just like we viewed the killing of George Floyd on the news. It was sickening and frightening to watch.

The police appear to have an abundance of employees who do not understand the difference between criminals and those citizens that they were hired to protect.

Why? National and organizational change is a double-edged sword. It can build a better society based on respect between the police and citizens – or it can unleash a new backlash from our citizenship. It can weed out those individual policemen and women who are unstable, hurtful, and even murderous or it can create the opposite chain-reaction. So, what is that elusive definitive resource for embracing change in our democracy? John Dunn wrote a book called *A History of Democracy*. In Chapter Four, called "Why Democracy," he said:

"It is tempting to believe that democracy has won its present eminence for either or both of two reasons. Some prefer to attribute its victory to its evident political justice, its being plainly the best, and perhaps the sole clearly justifiable basis on which human beings can accept the apparent indignity of being ruled at all. Others find it easier to believe that it owes this eminence to the fact that it and it alone can ensure the well-protected and fluent operation of a modern capitalist economy. Neither cheery view, unfortunately, can possibly be right. Democracy in itself, as we have seen, does not specify any clear and definite structure of rule. Even as an idea (let alone as a practical expedient) it wholly fails to ensure any regular and reassuring relationship to just outcomes over any issue at all. As a structure of rule, within any actual society at any time, it makes it overwhelmingly probable that many particular outcomes will turn out flagrantly unjust."

His words can be interpreted to mean that a democracy is bound to be turbulent on a regular basis. No sooner does one injustice raise its ugly head, but the next is already visible on the horizon. In 2020, we experienced an epic uncontrollable virus spread across the world. Due to our lack of decisive leadership, this disease crippled our economy, closed schools and businesses, and killed over half a million individuals – more deaths than any other nation. On the evening news this year, our nation witnessed the murder of yet another Black man at the hands of our police, resulting in massive demonstrations in large and small cities in every state. This man did not deserve to die – whatever crimes George Floyd committed in his life, none of them equated to being executed. It was unjustified.

We watched former President Trump be impeached for his unconstitutional behavior[4], yet he was not removed from office and continued to defame and disparage every individual who opposed him. In fact, he systematically set out to destroy the life of anyone who did not agree with him or approve of him. Trump misused his position of power and should have been impeached the first time around! Facts and corroborated testimony justified his impeachment, but Senate Republicans prevented justice. They failed our democracy!

President Putin of Russia, a man who former U.S. President Trump admires, rules Russia by eliminating any reporter who disparages him, he poisons his enemies or those who speak out against him (Alexei Navalny)[5] and arrests and falsely accuses, holds mock trials, and incarcerates individuals (Mikhail Khodorkovsky)[6] who stand in the way of his gaining resource power. Russians are accustomed to this type of inhumane leadership. Their society has adjusted so that they live in a "cautious" way.

In the old "Iron Curtain" days of Stalin, Khrushchev, and Brezhnev, people either joined the Communist Party or they were often imprisoned in Siberia. Gorbachev opened up Russia to the world and allowed people to live more freely. This period of freedom lasted less than one decade, which is only a blink in the thousands-of-years-long history of the Russian people. By the time Putin assumed power the curtain fell again – only this time it was not made of iron but of aluminum – a softer metal. The populace had changed, but the mentality of leadership had not. Putin, a former Soviet Military Intelligence Agent (KGB/FSU), still sees the United States as Russia's enemy.

Having lived in Russia both before and after the Soviet Empire ruled, I understood that just about everything I said and did was recorded. I also understood that as a foreigner, if I stayed in a hotel, there would be listening devices and often cameras hidden in the walls and ceiling. I changed my clothes in the bathroom with the lights off. While staying in a hotel in Kiev during this period, I stood next to the wall and clearly said, "Gee, I wish the hotel restaurant would serve oatmeal for breakfast." The next morning they served oatmeal for the first time. I learned who my primary "shadow" was and even knew who their substitutes were. In fact, one of the first KGB agents assigned to my family is now happily living in San Francisco with his wife and children.

After the iron curtain lifted, life in Russia and the former republics changed. My life, and that of ordinary Russians, was freer. By 1992, I had sold my home in Denver and moved to Moscow with my younger two children to work. My son was 13, and my youngest daughter was 12. I enrolled them in Moscow Public Schools, which were academically superior to similar schools in the U.S., and supplemented their instructions with private tutors. I remember my daughter saying, "Mom, I hope you know that I refuse to use this school's restrooms for an entire year." While the education was excellent, the Soviet-style school facilities were not modern by western standards.

Before choosing a school for my children to attend in Moscow, I interviewed three public schools. Each school invited me to sit in a classroom while the children discussed the history of the United States. These Russian children could describe how the U.S. flag was created, how many stars and stripes were found in the flag, and name the dates for flag changes – all in perfect English. In the United States you would never find a public school where the children could recite another country's history in a foreign language. Needless to say, I was impressed. My children quickly learned to speak Russian on a native level – including slang - due to their Russian friends and private tutors.

One KGB officer assigned to me and my family actually offered to let me view my file, which he described as five inches thick (12.7 centimeters in Russia). While helping other Americans negotiate a copper deal, I was invited to join the KGB. I was told that my ability to speak Russian and to enter the U.S. Embassy would be invaluable to the Russian government. Accepting such an invitation would be like signing a death warrant. So instead of agreeing, I spoke with an official who worked at the Ministry of Foreign Affairs and turned-in the man who had gleefully issued the KGB invitation. The last I heard, he lost his job.

Few Americans have become bi-cultural by moving from the U.S. to living in Russia or other former Soviet Republics. Conversely, there are thousands upon thousands of native Russians now living in the U.S. It is a far easier transition.

Leaving Russia, I spent several years working in Central Asia (five countries) and lived in both Almy Ata, Kazakhstan under President Nazarbaev, and in

Ashgabat, Turkmenistan under Turkmenbashi. I traveled throughout the region, including China, Iran, Iraq, India, Afghanistan, Pakistan and the other Central Asian countries. I was smuggled into Afghanistan during the first Taliban regime wearing a blue burqa as a disguise. My face was totally covered and I was provided "local" shoes to wear instead of my western-style shoes. While there, I was suddenly smacked on the back of my head with a rifle butt so hard that I fell to the dusty, dirty ground and cut my knee, not to mention the bump on the back of my skull. To deserve this treatment, I merely looked up instead of down at the ground.

The Taliban are ruthless killers.

Former U.S. Ambassador Bond and World Learning invited me to visit Bosnia as a consultant, and I was also invited to visit Rwanda by President Paul Kagame's office. I spent most of one year in Lima, Peru, working on a World Bank-funded project. I also worked with a World Bank project in Russia helping restructure large factories from a demand economy to a market economy.

"Market economies work using the forces of supply and demand to determine the appropriate prices and quantities for most goods and services in the economy."[7] The demand economies of the Soviet Union and then Russia were opposite to those of a market economy. "In the Soviet system, the government dictated economic policy, rather than relying on free market mechanisms and the law of supply and demand.[8] Soviet-type economic planning is the specific model of centralized planning employed by Marxist-Leninist socialist states,"[9] whereby the government decides what is manufactured and what other factory will purchase products.

Other consulting work included working with Vice President Moody in Kenya, where a retired American physician is still building birthing centers and health clinics due to the initial groundwork. These experiences provided insight and real-life understanding into governments and cultures other than the U.S. and our form of democracy.

Not long after Trump was sworn in as the U.S. President, he began criticizing the media. His behavior and words were similar to those I had experienced and heard in dictatorship countries. It was a loud and clear – and familiar - warning ringing in my ears. I was startled and alarmed, but more importantly, I felt frightened for all those Americans who did not recognize this warning. Millions of unassuming Americans just blindly believed Trump's election lies and many of these brainwashed individuals committed crimes on behalf of Trump.

> **Trump's words and behavior mirrored those of dictators.**

"Those who would give up essential Liberty, to purchase a little temporary safety, deserve neither Liberty nor Safety." – Benjamin Franklin[10]

"Dumb Man Walking," Artist – Pat Bagley, Courtesy of Cagle Cartoons.

Trump convinced his followers – many who unknowingly became domestic terrorists – using systematic repetition of a falsehood - that the Democrats had "stolen" the election from him while at the same time trying to convince the rest of the U.S. citizens that he had nothing to do with the Capitol riots. Both concepts were lies.

"Trump's Troops," Artist – Pat Bagley, Courtesy of Cagle Cartoons.

However, this is also what happens in dictator-lead countries where leader-induced violence is fueled by numerous reiteration of lies to crowds of individuals who can easily be manipulated. Echoing a lie does not make it the truth and the Democrats did not steal the election from Trump. He lost the election by about seven million votes.[11]

And in 2021, Putin secured his position of power. The Russian Duma passed a law permitting Putin to be the President of the Russian Federation until 2034. This happened solely because no one in the Russian Duma has the nerve to vote against Putin's wishes. Trump was well on his way to obtaining the same power with the help of the Republican majority in the U.S. Senate – this is dictator-type manipulation of elected government officials and lessons learned from Putin.

If you believe you are patriotic or a good "life-long" Republican by supporting Donald Trump, you were, in reality, helping him change our society from a democracy where every voice and vote counts into a repressive, autocratic nightmare. Do not believe his lies since every word spoken by Trump is about ego and self-preservation. His racist remarks sparked hatred, and he has even called the KKK (see page 8) "fine people." Come on, folks – the KKK are blood-thirsty racists who have murdered many innocent Black men, women, and children in cold blood. This is indisputable. They operate by instilling fear which is Trump's MO – mode of operation - and which he copied from President Putin.

No one was more of a Trump supporter than President Vladimir Putin in Russia. The assumed reason for this support was that Putin had already converted Trump so that he was controlled and directed by President Putin.

"Capitol Riots 2021," Artist – Alla and Chavdar, Courtesy of Cagle Cartoons.

The people who stormed the Capitol were led by lies and conspiracy theories fed to them by former President Trump and probably provided by Putin. The *New York Times* article written by Peter Baker and Sabrina Tavernise on Sunday, February 24, 2021 states:

"*The pure savagery of the mob that rampaged through the Capitol that day was breathtaking, as cataloged by the injuries inflicted on those who tried to guard the nation's lawmakers. These officer's injuries included the loss of one eye, loss of a tip of a finger, and loss of life. One officer was shocked so many times by a Taser that he had a heart attack... One of the Trump supporters read over a bullhorn one of the president's angry tweets to charge up the crowd.*" [12]

> **The truth is, Trump lost the election by millions of votes.**

13

Nick Bryant is the New York correspondent for the BBC. He wrote on November 7th, 2020[14]:

"*But the 2020 election was not a re-run of the 2016 election. This time he was the incumbent, not the insurgent. He had a record to defend, including his mishandling of a coronavirus outbreak which by Election Day had killed more than 230,000 Americans. In this age of negative partisanship, where politics is often driven by loathing of the opposition, he was not pitted against a hate figure like Hillary Clinton. They (voters) were put off by his aggressiveness. His stoking of racial tensions. His use of racist language in tweets maligning people of colour. His failure, on occasions, to adequately condemn White Supremacy. His trashing of America's traditional allies and his admiration for authoritarian strongmen, such as Vladimir Putin. His strange boasts about being "a very stable genius" and the like. His promotion of conspiracy theories. His use of a lingua franca that sometimes made him sound more like a crime boss, such as when he described his former lawyer Michael Cohen, who reached a plea deal with federal prosecutors, as "a rat".*

The U.S. election in November 2020 was reassuring. The vast majority of Americans voted Trump out of the White House and out of power and chose President Biden to assume the reigns of control. Biden had been a public servant for forty-four years. From 1973 to 2009 he served as a U.S. Senator, and then from 2009 to 2017 as the U.S. Vice President. He is knowledgeable, experienced, and qualified to hold the office of President of the United States. Trump was not qualified or competent. Democracy worked in this election before Trump could pass laws giving himself a lifetime of autocratic political control.

But no one knows what will happen in 2024, or if there is yet another individual similar to Trump who will run for the presidency and who can be manipulated by Putin, or will Putin be able to maneuver Trump into winning the Republican Presidency again?

Let's hope between 2021 and the election in 2024, the American public will be more educated and wiser about the tools used to disrupt our democracy such as: racism, violence, and hatred, including Trump's style of brain-washing.

If we are going to save our democracy, we must choose our leaders more carefully.

CHAPTER 4 – END NOTES

1 https://www.nytimes.com, "How George Floyd Was Killed in Police Custody," Written by Evan Hill, Ainara Tiefenthailer, Christiaan Triebert, Drew Jordan, Haley Willis and Robin Stein, May 31, 2020.

2 https://www.cnn.com, "Police probe clears Dayton, Ohio, officers who pulled paraplegic driver out of car," Written by Peter Nickeas and Amanda Watts, CNN, January 12, 2022.

3 https://www.nbcnews.com, "Buffalo police officers suspended after video shows them shoving an elderly man to the ground," Written by Tim Stelloh, Rima Abdelkader and Caitlin Fichtel., June 4, 2020.

4 https://www.congress.gov, H.Res.24 – "Impeaching Donald John Trump, President of the United States for high crimes and misdemeanors." January 25, 2021.

5 https://worldcrunch.com, "Yes, Navalny Still Matters, But Putin's Opposition Can't Fix Russia Now." Written by Sergei Karpukhin and Cameron Manley, January 18, 2023.

6 https://www.economist.com, "Mikhail Khodorkovsky on how to deal with the 'bandit' in the Kremlin," March 19, 2022.

7 https://www.investopedia.com, "What is a Market Economy and How Does it Work?", Written by The Investopedia Team, April 07, 2022.

8 https://socialsci.libretexts.org, , Written by Caitlin Finlayson at the University of Washington. August 16, 2020.

9 https://wikipedia, "Soviet-type economic planning."

10 NPR, "Ben Franklin's Famous 'Liberty, Safety' Quote Lost its Context in 21st Century," March 2, 2015.

11 https://www.cnn.com. "Biden's popular vote margin over Trump tops 7 million votes." Written by Kate Sullivan and Jennifer Agiesta, December 4, 2020.

12 The New York Times, "January 6 United States Capitol Attack," Written by Peter Baker and Sabrina Tavernise, February 24, 2021.

13 USA Today, Fact Check: "Trump lost the 2020 presidential election by about seven million votes," Written by Ella Lee, December 8, 2020.

14 Httsp://www.ussc.edu.au, "A conversation with author Nick Bryant and his article in the NYT", November 7, 2020.

Chapter Five

U.S. Democracy vs. Communism

" **C** ommunis_ (from Latin communis, "common, universal") is a philo-sophical, social, political, economic ideology and movement whose ultimate goal is the establishment of a communist society, namely a socioeconomic order structured upon the ideas of common ownership of the means of production and the absence of social classes, money and the state." [1] Of course this definition does not reflect the daily real-world life of people living under communism or a dictatorship. The concept of "common ownership" is not authentic. Only the wealthy or those in power rule - and those not in power, needed a relative, friend, or neighbor who is "powerful" as a Godfather to protect and support them.

An example of this would be car ownership in a Communist system. In the old days, you needed to put your name on a list and wait about two years before you could receive a new car. You had no choice of the color. In the 1990's, I was working and living in Moscow. I had several friends in rather high government positions including the Deputy Director of Finance. When I told Yuri that I really missed driving a car (he had driven with me when he was in Denver, CO.), he offered to sell his Lada to me and I jumped on his offer. He picked me up at my apartment and drove me to the office of the local Russian "DMV". There was a very long line at this building ending somewhere around the block. Yuri and I went inside, met with the District Manager who already had my papers prepared. He had decided that I needed a Russian license plate and not one for a foreign resident. He explained to me that there are young men in Moscow who drive around and deliberately hit cars with foreign license plates and then bribe them with not reporting the accident which was always recorded as the foreigners fault and the foreigner would be held responsible for all accident-associated costs. Also, at this time there were very few women driving cars in Moscow. After six months of driving in Moscow – and I love to drive in the U.S. – I threw up my arms and sold the car. Gas stations called "benzokolonka" were hard to find. They were tucked under various buildings and not on street corners like in the U.S. When the car needed repair, I was told to allow a male to help because the repairmen would not talk to a woman or charge twice the cost. Last, the car alarm would go off in the middle of the night. By the time I would be dressed and on my way out into the freezing Moscow winter nights to turn off the alarm, neighbors in my building would be looking out their windows to see whose noisy car had been the culprit. Owning a car in Moscow was not what I had expected.

The Russian form of government differs from Chinese communism in many ways. One major difference is that the Chinese leadership wants the world to think well of them and their country, while the Russian leadership simply does not care what the world thinks of them. The Chinese government believes it is "maneuvering and manipulating" other countries through their deceptive global marketing efforts. Russians are far more calculating.

In the book called *Russian Roulette*, on page 59, Isikoff and Corn stated:

"For years, U.S. officials had been grappling with Russian cyber intrusions. As far back as 1996, Russian hackers penetrated Defense Department networks and stole documents that if piled up would be three times the height of the Washington Monument. In the 2000s, the Chinese were perceived as the biggest cyber threat to the United States – they were stealing data from government data- bases and American companies practically at will . . . but the Chinese were noisy about it. They left readily identifiable fingerprints. Ledgett (former head of the National Security Agency) had long since become convinced the Russians were the more sophisticated

and stealthy adversary . . . "the Chinese would break into your house, smash the windows and steal your cutlery," he later explained. "The Russians would pick your lock, reset the alarm, and steal the last five checks in your checkbook so you wouldn't even know they were there."

The reason that Russians excel at playing chess is because they think strategically, analytically, and instinctually from the time they are toddlers. This skill is ingrained and perhaps is the primary reason that most Americans or others cannot truly understand Russia.

Democracy, on the other hand, is defined as, "Democracy (Greek: δημοκρατία, dēmokratiā, from dēmos 'people' and kratos 'rule') a form of government in which the people have the authority to choose their governing legislation. Who people are and how authority is shared among them are core issues for democratic theory, development, and constitution." [2] This definition, too, does not reflect real life in a democracy. Again, only those in power or who are wealthy rule.

As an American who studied Russia and Russian for many years, then lived and worked in the Soviet Union and then Russia in the late 1980s, the 1990s, and part of the 2000s, I witnessed and personally experienced communism and dictatorship. Today in 2021, Russia calls its form of government a socialist state with free elections. In reality, it is a dictatorship with an autocratic leader who has ruled this vast country and its people since 2000. Putin will not relinquish his power, and controls Russia by implementing various frightening methodologies of control.

"Putin For Power," Artist – Paresh Nath, Courtesy of Cagle Cartoons.

"The Russian 616-member parliament, termed the Federal Assembly, consists of two houses – the 450-member State DUMA (the lower house) and the 166-member Federation Council (the upper house). The DUMA is made up of elected officials from the various regions of Russia who hold office for five years."[3] However, just like the Republicans in the U.S. Senate, no member of the lower or upper houses will vote or speak against any initiative proposed by Putin. Thus, Russia's government is solidly grounded in autocratic life-threatening fear.

> **The United States has now tasted this same form of governance and witnessed the exact same phobias by US elected officials in Washington DC.**

Russia is a fascinating country with a history that spans thousands of years. The chopping block used by Ivan the Terrible is still standing in Red Square.[4] He was the first Tsar of Russia from 1547 to 1584.[5] This "block" is a large circular-white stone stage upon which he beheaded his enemies. Other stories say that he announced the beheading while standing on this stage, but actually performed the beheading behind St. Basil's Cathedral. Not to be outdone, the Romanovs (the House of Romanov from 1613 to 1917)[6] converted Russia into a lavish competitor of the opulent homes found in Europe. Czar Alexander and Czarina Katherine built magnificent castles. Their winter home is now the Hermitage Museum. [7] The favorite residence of Czar Peter I (Peter the Great), located along the northern coast not far from St. Petersburg, surpassed the gardens of Versailles in France for elaborate, grandiose impressions. There are over one hundred gigantic gold statues and fountains greeting visitors throughout the gardens.[8]

The Hermitage Museum, established in 1764 and located at Thirty-Eight Palace Embankment, St. Petersburg,[9] houses some of the world's most famous artist's paintings and porcelains. This includes artwork by Da Vinci, Raphael, Caravaggio, Michelangelo, and even Picasso.

If you are an art lover and planning a trip to Russia, the Hermitage Museum richly articulates the history of St. Petersburg, of Russia, of the Czars, and the elaborate architecture indicative of old-world Russia. I worked and lived in St. Petersburg for several years and lived near Nevsky Prospect and the Fontanka Canal. Daily, I walked my borzoi near the Hermitage Museum, the only area nearby with a lawn.

Immediately after World War I (1914 to 1918)[10] and the 1917 Revolution[11] in Russia, the country was engulfed in a civil war, famine, and the teachings of Karl Marx and then Vladimir Lenin. Unknown to many Americans, Karl Marx's "social theory was one the great intellectual achievements of the nineteenth century - often compared with Darwin's *Theory of Evolution*." [12]

By 1921 through 1928, Lenin's New Economic Policies were enacted and the Soviet Union was formed in 1922.[13] Lenin died in 1924[14] and left his new government to the evil dictatorship of Joseph Stalin, who ruled the Soviet Union until 1953.[15] "Stalin was responsible for transforming a peasant society into a military and industrial power, but he ruled by terror and killed millions of his own citizens, mostly by starvation. He cut off the delivery of food and supplies to specific regions, like the vast territory of Ukraine, which resulted in the cruel, slow deaths of millions of souls."[16] World War II spanned the years from 1939 to 1945, and the "Cold War era" began in 1947 shortly after WWII.[17] Stalin's death in 1953 was followed by Communist leaders[18] who followed Stalin's "dictatorship model of leadership. This includes Khrushchev (1955 to 1964), Brezhnev (1964 to 1982), and then Gorbachev (1985 to 1991). Yeltsin was the first Russian President (1991 to 1999) and Putin was the second. Putin's style of leadership is comparable to Stalin's by many in Russia.

Gorbachev was the Russian leader who created the Soviet Union's new relationship with the outside world; he opened up the society to democratic concepts called perestroika and glasnost; and he set the stage for the collapse of the Soviet Union in the early 1990s. President Gorbachev and his family were in the Crimea on vacation and were totally isolated during the August Coup. There was fear that he and his family would be murdered, much like the Romanoff's.

©Taylor Jones - Hoover Digest   caglecartoons.com

"The Russian Evolution," Artist – Taylor Jones, Courtesy of Cagle Cartoons.

By the time Yeltsin took control of Russia, the doors opened to western businesses, and Russian citizens were allowed to leave the country. International travel was previously a privilege denied to most citizens. When Yeltsin assumed control of Russia, I had been doing business (for the U.S. Government) there for several years and had made the transition to be bi-cultural.

The Russian constitutional crisis of 1993 was due to a political clash between President Yeltsin and the Russian Parliament (DUMA). Much like the violence instigated by Donald Trump on January 6, 2021, Yeltsin staged a coup, bombed the Russian White House which crushed the revolt, and resolved their ongoing power struggle. Yeltsin won. Russia continued to be led by a dictator. Trump also attempted a coup in order to retain his power. He lost.

My fourteen-year-old son, along with his Russian friends – all children of active KGB personnel - stood on the bridge over the Moscow River and watched as Yeltsin ordered large artillery fire into the Russian "White House." It was this coup that triggered the continuation of Russia as a dictatorship government – but it did not end the Cold War.

There have been many books written that describe the Russian society before and after Yeltsin. Hedrick Smith wrote *The Russians* in 1976 and *The New Russians* in 1991. Jeffrey Tayler wrote *Siberian Dawn* in 1999. Jeff was fluent in Russian and had worked as a translator for Radio Free Europe and afterward for the Peace Corps. This book is about an American (Jeff) who literally hitchhiked across the "new Russia" with $900 in his pocket. He stayed at my Moscow apartment before his journey across Russia and again afterward. It is difficult to imagine his trip in a country three times larger than the United States with poor, underdeveloped, muddy, or frozen roads that are nearly impossible to travel in any vehicle during most of the year. His book does an excellent job describing Russia and Russians.

During this era, Moscow saw an infiltration of American businesses – McDonald's, Pizza Hut, Taco Bell, and notably, the Beverly Hills night club, restaurant, and casino, half-owned by Chuck Norris (the American movie star) and the other half owned by Mayor Lyushkov of Moscow. "Those who attended the casino's grand opening included Donald Trump, Las Vegas Mayor Jan Laverty Jones, and of course Chuck Norris. Contemporaries remembered the Beverly Hills casino as one of the most criminalized and dangerous gambling venues in Moscow."[19]

My oldest daughter, Lize, was the manager of this joint venture. It was her responsibility to accurately record the white and the black books (accounting records). Most businesses in Russia kept accurate business records (black books) and also books for government accounting audits (white books). At this time, it was impossible to operate a successful and profitable business due to the unrealistic Russian tax laws. Western retail outlets flooded Moscow and St. Petersburg streets, and western automobiles were sold in used car lots – many of which were owned by ex-Soviet Union employees who had lost their jobs. These same individuals often opened small banks with money smuggled from the USSR and from bank accounts abroad. They had assistance from Russians living in New York or other large American cities where USSR monies had been stashed.

This stage in Russian history was affectionately known as the "wild west" period.[20] Many Americans scrambled to form joint ventures with their Russian counterparts. Naïve and under-educated about Russia, people like Chuck Norris lost mega investment dollars when Mayor Lyushkov decided to tear up the joint venture documents and prevented Norris from returning to Russia. Chuck Norris was lucky that all he lost was money. Many other Americans and foreigners were murdered.

Afterward, my daughter was threatened by the newly appointed Russian manager of the Beverly Hills. She ended up smuggling some of the joint venture records out of Russia by an overnight train to Helsinki. Those records were stowed in a Chandler, Arizona storage unit for roughly twenty years until her death in 2016 when I destroyed them.

Lize died in Japan in 2016. The Tokyo Police ruled her death a homicide. There is also evidence that it was either an accidental drug overdose or a poisoning. Poisoning is a standard murder method used by Russian mafia. One trait of Russians is their ability to be patient, to be vengeful, and to "get even." Considering her association with some of the toughest men in Russia, nothing would surprise me, but then nothing will bring her back. I morn her loss daily and will always feel responsible.

Paul Tatum from Oklahoma was another American in Russia.[21] He became joint venture partners with a Chechen businessman named Umar Dzhabrailov, and together they opened the first American upscale hotel in Moscow called the Radisson Slavyanskaya. In a battle with his partner to control the hotel, Paul took out a full-page newspaper ad stating his legal case against Dzhabrailov and Mayor

Luzhkov. I attempted to warn Paul - as did others - but like many foreigners in Russia, he did not understand that western rules, laws, and logic did not apply to the Russian business environment. A few weeks after this ad was published, Paul was gunned down and killed in a subway entrance. He had hired ten Russian bodyguards, but none came to his rescue. They all followed him and walked down the first set of subway steps, but when they reached the first landing, his bodyguards went back up and Paul went down to his death. While bodyguards in Russia – and the whole former USSR and surrounding countries - received good salaries, their loyalty was to their families who may have been threatened in advance of such a murder.

As a security consultant to the International Rescue Committee (IRC) in the early 2000's, I was flown to New York to discuss the murders of their foreign staff in Afghanistan. The IRC had hired a local Afghan as head of security. As previously mentioned, local employees can be vulnerable and their families/children exposed, hurt, or killed if they do not aid in killing foreigners or other crimes. While this is a simple truth, many Americans living and/or working abroad do not grasp this reality. When I explained this to the IRC senior staff in New York, they simply did not believe that their Afghan Head of Security would do such a thing. My response was to ask them what they would do if their children lives had been threatened?

I have found that most American business men and women, do not understand life, business, politics or much outside of the United States. I know this because at one point in my life, I also thought that I knew more than I did. To become bi-cultural from the United States to Russia is a multi-year process of trial and error – to give up the American materialism and arrogance, and relearn how to survive in a totally criminal world.

CNN recently (September 10, 2021) aired a show called "What Went Wrong in Afghanistan."[22] American history has repeated this same story over and over. As Americans, we impose our beliefs, our ways of thinking, and our form of government on other societies and then are surprised when they do not respond as we envisioned. The Taliban told the American government and military personnel that there would be law and order in the country and no one would be hurt.[23] Less than a week after the U.S. totally withdrew from Afghanistan, the Taliban beheaded a local police officer and then paraded his bleeding, severed head around the streets of Kabul.[24]

During the fall of the Afghan government (August 2021) and the brutal takeover by the Taliban, ISIS staged a suicide bombing that killed thirteen Americans and over 170 Afghan citizens (this number varies) trying to escape the country.[25] American officials appeared to be surprised and many said that the Taliban airport security failed. I don't believe it failed. This bombing was probably orchestrated between the Taliban and ISIS – even though they are also adversaries. There was no mention on international news about Taliban fighters dying during this horrific attack. ISIS and ISIS-K have a stronghold in northern Afghanistan and wish to continue their own form of terrorism. ISIS is more prone to bombings than the Taliban, who terrorize innocent citizens – through torture and murder - in order force them to conform to their perverted version of Islam.

The *Moscow Business Survival Guide (early 1990's)* published a helpful hint for Westerners who dared to work in Russia – or anywhere in this region. It says, "The most fundamental concepts that have guided your judgment for a lifetime are not even known, much less understood here." Russians and the Russian way of life are radically different from life in the United States and the West. Becoming bi-cultural from the U.S. to Russia is a process of giving up all preconceived thought processes until you can "think and navigate" as a Russian. Russians think three-dimensionally – a concept that is often difficult to explain to Westerners.

Having lived under the oppressive orthodoxy of Communism and having witnessed numerous frightening lessons on how Soviet official egoism and bureaucracy work, my life profoundly changed. Figuratively speaking, I transformed from an innocent (American) naive child and grew into an educated and wiser (Russian) adult. I became reasonably fearful of those individuals in influential and prominent positions and intimately and distinctly knowledgeable of every aspect of Russian life. I thought, looked like, spoke, and behaved like a Russian.

This transformation often saved my life, and this hard-earned aptitude also resulted in a knack to fully recognize the very real danger of Trump's words and actions. That, combined with the hatred propagated by Trump every time a microphone came close to his face, and the preventable deaths of many Blacks in the U.S., is why this book was written. Trump was not directly responsible for the death of George Floyd, but he should be directly accountable for the racial hatred and lies which he openly communicated to the U.S. public, and which instigates deadly violence. Watching U.S. violence, hatred, and political chaos on Russian television is one of those rare moments when Putin laughs.[26]

Much like the Russian leadership, Trump continuously conveyed misinformation to the U.S. public as a perversion of reality. Also like Putin, Trump has attempted to gain control of media sources to promote his misinformation. There were reports that he even used an international marketing firm (Israel) called Psy-Group[27], an organization known to create and distribute fake news and augmenting it through a network of more than 5,000 fake social media accounts.

Catherine Belton wrote *Putin's People*, a lengthy book published both in the U.K. and in the U.S. in 2020. Catherine directly interviewed many Russians to obtain her information which includes the details about: (1) Russian interference in the U.S. elections (which the Russians later confessed to)[28] (2) Trump's bankruptcies and his ties to many Russians, and (3) how Russians working for the KGB hooked Trump and then appeared to have bribed him when he became President of the U.S.

Catherine was an investigative journalist for *Reuters* based in Moscow and also worked for the *Moscow Times*, the *Financial Times*, and *Business Week*. She says:

"*This book began as an effort to trace the takeover of the Russian economy by Putin's former KGB associates. But it became an investigation into something more pernicious than that. First research – and then events – showed that the kleptocracy of the Putin era was aimed at something more than just filling the pockets of the president's friends. What emerged as a result of the KGB takeover of the economy – and the country's political and legal system – was a regime in which the billions of dollars at Putin's cronies' disposal were to be actively used to undermine and corrupt the institutions and democracies of the West." (p. 15, Putin's People).*

She goes on to say:

"Donald Trump met Shalva Tcfhigirinsky in 1990. Some of the people tied to Tchigirinsky included a Georgian, Tamir Sapin, his business partner Sam Kislin, and an Azeri Aras Agalarov who set up some of the first Soviet-American joint ventures and U.S. trading operations before the Soviet fall. They were part of an interconnecting web of figures that became testimony to the enduring power of the black-cash networks created in the final years of the Communist regime. Some of them later joined Trump in real-estate ventures, helping bail him out when he fell into financial difficulty, offering the prospect of lucrative construction deals in Moscow, while Agalarov organized the 2013 Miss Universe pageant in Moscow. They were among those who, according to Yury Shvets, 'later helped save Trump from bankruptcy.' (p. 451, Putin's People)."

Trump was obviously indebted to these Russians and has been associated with many Russians, some as early as 1990. Dmitry Rybolovlev[29] and Oleg Deripaska[30] are among Trump's Russian connections. In fact, Deripaska was recently arrested (November 2021) by the FBI in Washington, D.C. with issues related to the 2016 Trump campaign. Both these men were involved in the Christi auction of the supposedly daVinci painting called Salvator Mundi[31] along with two Saudi's who purposely outbid each other possibly to laundry money. This painting has since disappeared.[32] Rybolovlev bought a Trump Palm Beach home for $100 million[33] (he later demolished the property) which was purchased by Trump four years earlier for $40 million. The Mueller investigation suggested that this purchase was to save Trump from another bankruptcy. The question is why? In 2016, Trump reportedly met twice with Rybolovlev just before the U.S. election.[34]

Anna Politkovskaya[35] "was a fearless critic of the powerful people in the new Russia. She wrote *Putin's Russia*, which was originally published in London in 2004. This book was never published, translated, or distributed in Russia, but it tells an accurate and chilling story of Putin's rise to power. It provides Westerners an account of how this autocratic, Soviet-style dictator systematically eliminates his opponents and reporters not favorable to him. Anna was murdered in October 2006 at the age of 48 while reporting on the Russian war in Chechnya and writing a scorching account of Vladimir Putin."

Putin has guided the new Russia into a world economic powerhouse by confiscating all natural resources and assuming power over Western joint ventures. Many "new" Russians are grateful that he has rebuilt their military might and restored pride in "Mother Russia" after Yeltsin, but many of his tactics resemble Stalin's merciless behavior. Most reputable scholars and historians estimate that the number of people Stalin killed was at least twenty million.[36] By contrast, when historians refer to Hitler, they often quote that six million Jews were murdered. In comparing ruthless leaders worldwide, there are few to none that are equivalent to Stalin. This is relevant because President Putin has been compared to Stalin – and Putin's leadership has been emulated and admired by Trump.

In the year 2020, the United States had a U.S. President that appeared to appreciate Putin's (Russia's) governing style more than the representative government of the U.S. democracy. He ignored expert medical advice, provided distorted truths to the American public about COVID, and then showed no concern for the hundreds of thousands of Americans dying of this disease.

During Trump's four years, the U.S. was struggling with a global deadly pandemic, with economic hardships and growing massive debt, with natural disasters, with police brutality and murders of innocent citizens, with escalating violence in every major city (in 2020, violence increased by 30% across the U.S.)[37], AND with a President who was sitting in the White House who had been impeached – TWICE. Yes, there is something drastically wrong with this picture!

There have been many investigations concerning this past President and his behavior. Trump calls these investigations "witch hunts," but each and every one of them were based on true evidence and factual information. Trump would like the American public to believe that those investigations were politically motivated to gain sympathy or support – but he was being investigated because the evidence clearly demonstrated that he disregarded the law.

"Trump Calls Grand Jury a Witch Hunt," Artist – Phil Hands.

Recent books written and published regarding Trump include: *The Room Where It Happened* by John Bolton, the former National Security Advisor of the United States. It is a good but long read. This book was written by a man who worked closely with Trump daily and explained the illogical and egocentric character of Trump's management. *Too Much and Never Enough* is a book written by Mary Trump, Ph.D. The cover says, "How my family created the world's most dangerous man." She has known Donald Trump since her childhood. Both these authors intimately know him better than you or I.

In 2020, we witnessed the inhumane murder of another Black man at the hands of police. This time it was recorded and televised to the entire country and around the world. This event prompted an onslaught of new books on racism. Robin DiAngelo wrote *WhiteFragility*, with the subtitle "Why it's so hard for

White people to talk about racism." One of my favorites is *Surrender, White People,* authored by D.L. Hughley and Doug Moe. Another excellent book was written by Don Lemon, a CNN anchor. His book is named *This is the Fire* where he opens the debate concerning race issues in the U.S.

Democracy represents the people who have the right to vote and decide their governing legislators. Cornerstones of democracy are freedom of speech and assembly, equality, and self-determination. It is a form of government designed to protect the innocent, the minorities, the disabled, the aged, and all others – a citizenship.

> **In the year 2020 under Trump's Presidency, our nation was not working for the people and by the people, and was not a functioning democracy.**

Non-violent protestors exercising their freedom to assemble and speak were met with tear gas and federal military troops ordered by Trump. Minorities are not protected, but are murdered and beaten by police. Several former Trump employees have gone to prison. Trump "buddies" who were guilty of more serious crimes were pardoned or released from prison. Perhaps most importantly, the balance of power our forefathers created was not working as witnessed by our entire nation when Trump violated constitutional law and was twice impeached by the House of Representatives on factual proof but was not convicted by the Senate. If you have not asked why this happened, then you need to.

The Russian Duma operates the same as the Republican Senate from 2016 to 2020. They recently created a law that gave Putin the right to govern Russia basically for the rest of his life. Then in turn, he will select the next leader who will mirror his values. The U.S. Senate and their Republican leadership who refused to vote against Trump on any issue, could have passed a similar law that gave Trump that same type of power. Of course, it would require a constitutional amendment and ratification by the states (22nd Amendment).[38] If this happened, our democracy would have died in 2020.

Our way of life is struggling to survive, and no one knows if our democratic society and government will endure. Trump was impeached in the House on charges related to pressuring Ukraine to investigate Joe Biden and his son. Trump openly admitted on national TV to withholding badly needed and Senate-approved military financial aid to Ukraine in their fight against Russia's aggression because he did not want to anger President Putin.[39] Why?

Trump was acquitted in the Senate due to partisanship instead of our elected officials following the factual truth. Almost every Republican in the Senate was afraid of Trump and his bullying tactics. Ohio Representative Anthony Gonzales (R) was one of the ten House Republicans who voted to impeach President Trump. This elected official now has 24-hour armed protection, fears for his family's safety, and will not run for re-election.[40] This same dynamic is found in the Russian Duma, where every single elected official in the Duma supports Putin knowing themselves, or a member of their family will end up dead, poisoned, or in prison if they don't.

> **The comparison is impossible to ignore.**
> **WAKE UP AMERICA!**

Trump fired or threatened any person in his administration that was not an avid or loyal supporter. In fact, he is obsessive about loyalty. For example, he fired two directors of National Intelligence, Dan Coates and Joseph Maguire,[41] for issues related to Russia's interference in the 2016 election. As a result, there has NEVER been a counter-intelligence investigation into Trump's relationship with Russia. This book helps to fill-in the gaps not investigated by the U.S. Government regarding Trump and Russia.

Did you ever wonder why Russians ostensibly celebrated Trump's win in 2016? There are several theories. First and foremost is that Putin strongly disliked

Hilary Clinton, and therefore did not want her to win. He wanted revenge because Hilary Clinton had openly expressed her dislike for Putin (the same type of begrudging behavior we have seen from Trump.) Russians hold grudges for years, then retaliate. Second, is a theory passed along by several close long-time Russian personal friends. The story is that when Trump traveled to Moscow, he didn't realize that his hotel room was fitted with listening devices and cameras.

Most foreigners who visit Russia never see or learn of their hotel room's "extra amenities," but every single hotel room in Russia where a foreigner stays has spying devices. Foreigner's hotel rooms also have prostitutes knocking on the hotel room door or calling the room to offer services – sometimes all night. This was especially true in any hotel room used by visiting dignitaries.

Trump is well known for his lust for attractive women, and Russian prostitutes are breathtakingly beautiful. Few know the whole truth about what was recorded or videotaped, but apparently, it was enough for Putin to "maneuver" Trump into the position of President of the United States of America and then provide him with Russia's "wish list" – their demands. So, for the average Russian on the street in Moscow, there is little doubt that Trump won the 2016 election due to Russia's interference and that Russia will continue to do so because it is in Putin's interest. Vladimir Putin was/still is an excellent Russian secret service agent who knows how to manipulate his subjects.

"Donald Trump and NBC each made $2.3 million on the 2013 Miss Universe pageant, in part due to a big investment from a billionaire Russian family believed to have assisted with interference in the 2016 election, The Times reported that the most successful year for Miss Universe — both for Trump and its broadcaster, NBC — was in 2013, when the global pageant was held in Moscow. That pageant has become a key event for those investigating Trump's ties to Russia as Trump received help from Aras Agalarov — a billionaire who claims to have connections to Vladimir Putin — and his son, Emin. The event was held at Crocus City Hall, a venue owned by Agalarov, with Emin and his wife appearing respectively as a singer and a judge at the pageant." [42]

> **Trump does have close ties to Russia, and to individuals who are among Russia's most ruthless businessmen.**

Trump has repeatedly denied his personal relationships with the Russian "mafia" and/or government. Aras Agalarov[43], originally from Baku, Azerbaijan, moved to Moscow and founded a company called Crocus International. Trump's ties to the Russian criminal underworld – known in the West as the "Russian mafia" are incontrovertible. No business person in Russia becomes wealthy without such connections. All decisions in Russia are from the TOP down. Putin has complete control of Russia. Agalarov's estimated wealth is among the top individuals in Russia. Agalarov is just one among the many ties Trump has to Russia.

Catherine Belton states:

Agalarov appeared to be another of the agents recruited by the KGB in the twilight years of the Soviet Union to funnel cash into the West. (According to an interview with Yury Shvets.) In those days, any American joint venture could be established only with KGB approval, said Shvets. . . . Agalarov had also acquired a stake in Europe's biggest outdoor market called the Cherkizovsky Rynok . . . Agalorov's co-owners of the market included other Azeri associates including Tevfiq Arif, the former Soviet trade official who later bankrolled the construction of the Trump Tower in SoHo (which is in New York). (Page 457, Putin's People).

There is no uncertainty among Russians, or at least those who risk speaking on this subject, that Trump has been responding to Putin's whims. Trump's treatment of NATO, his withdrawal of American troops from Germany and Libya, and his position on Afghanistan were all on Putin's "demand list." Remember, too, it was Trump who initiated the U.S. troop withdrawal from Afghanistan.

Trump's constant and often vulgar criticism of any Democrat, anyone else not loyal to him, or anyone who is not White and rich, has fed divisions in our country. Violence has soared in many major cities[44] – some increases have been over 100%.

This list includes New York, Chicago, Washington, D.C., Atlanta, Los Angeles, Portland, and others. (FBI Crime Data Base for 2020).

In addition, Trump attempted to stop mail-in voting, claiming that it was fraudulent.[45] Due to Trump's term in office, the United States Postal Service has announced it's slow down of mail delivery and its increase of all postage costs. In the year 2021, the post office will be operating as if it is still the 1970s.

For the first time in U.S. history, we saw a President snub his successor and refuse to accept his loss, namely because his ego was bruised, or possibly because of his dread of Putin' wrath. He has every reason to be fearful of Putin.

So, voters of America – the choice is yours. Either you join the many Republicans who still believe that the 2020 election was not legitimate – a LIE - or believe the FACTS pointing in the opposite direction.

There were millions of German voters who did the same thing. They blindly believed in a leader who was fanatical. Look at what that history lesson taught. My fear is that the lessons of Auschwitz were so long ago that people have forgotten. Let me remind you.

"The Holocaust, also known as the Shoah, was the genocide of European Jews during World War II. Between 1941 and 1945, Nazi Germany and its collaborators systematically murdered some six million Jews across German-occupied Europe, around two-thirds of Europe's Jewish population. The murders were carried out in pogroms and mass shootings; by a policy of extermination through labor camps and gas chambers."[46]

Yes, six million human beings were tortured and murdered by Hitler. Three times as many lives were lost when Stalin ruled Russia. The statistics for Putin have not yet been calculated, but his governing style has been compared to Stalin's.[47] As of 2022, more than one million Americans so far have lost their battle with COVID-19 most likely due to Trump's lack of management of this disease.[48] This loss of life is continuing at an alarming rate because many Americans are not vaccinated and they continue to believe Trump's lies instead of the advice of educated and knowledgeable physicians, scientists, and experts.

Listen to the medical experts and not the politicians.

CHAPTER 5 – END NOTES

1 https://cn.wikipedia.org/wiki/Communism.

2 https://www.merriam-webster.com.

3 http://russiangovernment.ru and http://duma.gov.ru.

4 https://izi.travel_7796-the-execution-place

5 https://courses.lumenlerning.com_chapter-Ivan-the-terrible.

6 https://www.townandcountrymag.com. "The Devastating True Story of the Romanov Family Rule and Executiion."

7 Petrohof, a book written by Vadim Znamehof, published in Russian in 2003.

8 Ibid.

9 Saint Petersburg, A book published in Russian and printed and bound in Russia, narrative written by Natalia Popova and Andrei Fedorov, 2002.

10 https://en.wikipedia.org_wiki_World-War-I.

11 https://en.wikipedia.org_wiki_Russian-Revolution.

12 https://simplysociology.com_socialogical-theories, "Karl Marx's Sociological Theory, by Guy Evans. "The basic idea of Marx's theory is that society is characterized by the struggle between the workers and those in charge."

13 https://www.history.com. "On December 30, 1922, in post-revolutionary Russia, the Union of Soviet Socialist Republics (USSR) was established, comprising a confederation of Russia, Belorussia, Ukraine and the Transcaucasian Federation (divided in 1936 into the Georgian, Azerbaijan, and Armenian republics)."

14 https://www.karger.com. Lenin died on January 21, 1924 at the age of 53.

15 https://en.wikipedia.org_wiki_Joseph-Stalin. He held power as General Secretary of the Communist Party of the Soviet Union from 1922 to 1952 and Chairman of the Council of Ministers of the Soviet Union from 1941 to 1953. Initially governing the country as part of a collective leadership, he consolidated power to become a dictator by the 1930s.

16 https://cia.umn.edu. Holocaust and Genocide Studies. "In 1932 and 1933, millions of Ukrainians were killed in the Holodomor, a man-made famine engineered by the Soviet government of Joseph Stalin."

17 https://timetoast.com_timeline_wwii_cold-war.

18 https:/en.wikipedia.org_wiki_List-of-leaders-of-the-Soviet-Union. A List of Leaders of the Soviet Union.

19 Russia Beyond (in English), "Ten Casinos that Ruled Moscow," Written by Vitaly Arutyunov.

20 https://www.moderntimes.review. "The Russia of the 90's is frequently referred to as a 'Wild West.' It's sudden transition from communism to free-market capitalism was brutally rocky and on an uncharted path."

21 https://gangstersinc.org_an-american-businessman-in-Moscow. "The Story of Paul Tatum," Paul Tatum and The Moscow City Government had a quiet working relationship for two years. After that time, it started to rumble.

22 https://carnegieendowment.org, 2021/11/09. "Aiding Afghan Local Governance: What Went Wrong? False Assumptions About Communication and Linkages. Written by Frances Z. Brown, November 8, 2021.

23 https://www.usip.org. "Establishing the Rule of Law in Afghanistan." "In most of Afghanistan, the rule of law has never been strong, but after 23 years of warfare it has been displaced almost completely by the 'rule of the gun."

24 https://www.youtube.com. "Taliban beheads local Afghan police officer in a chilling video." September 12, 2021.

25 https://npr.org. "Kabul Airport Attack: 13 U.S. Service Members Killed." August 26, 2021.

26 https://www.bbc.com. "Putin laughs at political chaos in the U.S., especially concerning Trump's alleged relationship with Russia.", 18 may 2017.

27 https://en.wikipedia.org. "Psy-Group is a former Israeli private intelligence agency." "Highly skilled in operating in complex and challenging environments, PSY's intelligence team has a proven track record in information gathering, analysis, etc. They supposedly developed a covert pro-Trump plan and attempted to influence at least one US election."

28 https:www.reuters.com/world/Russia-prigozhin. "Russia's Prigozhin admits interfering in U.S. elections." November 7, 2022.

29 https://www.nytimes.com. "The Billionaire Who Bought Trump's Mansion Faces Scrutiny..." September 7, 2018.

30 https://www.theguardian.com. "Is Oleg Deripaska the missing link in the Trump-Russia Investigation? Trump lifts sanctions on firms linked to Russian oligarch Oleg Deripaska." January 29, 2019.

31 https://wwwnews.;artnet.com. "7 Unbelievable and Contentious Takeaways from the New Documentary About 'Salvator Mundi,' the $450 Million 'Lost Leonardo." August 27, 2021.

32 https://news.artnet.com. "Where in the World Is 'Salvator Mundi'?" Written by Kenny Schachter, June 10, 2019.

33 https://www.newswekk.com. "Trump sold a $40 million estate to a Russian Oligarch for $100 Million ...", Written by Tom Porter, February 10, 2018.

34 https://www.businessinsider.com, "White House Denounces "Conspiracy' on Trump, Rybolovlev the Russian Billionaire. A private plane owned by a Russian oligarch who has ties to Donald Trump and his secretary of commerce flew into cities where Trump was campaigning before the November election at least twice, flight data and photographs have shown. Written by Natasha Bertrand, March 7, 2017.

35 The Guardian, reported on 5 October 2018.

36 https://en.wikipedia.org/wiki. "Excess mortality in the Soviet Union under Joseph Stalin. "Prior to the dissolution of the Soviet Union and the archival revelations, some historians estimated that the numbers killed by Stalin's regime were 20 million or higher."

37 https://pewresearch.org. "What we know about the increase in U.S. murders in 2020. "The U.S. murder rate rose 30% between 209 and 2020 – the largest single=year increase in more than a century." October 27, 2021.

38 https://consititution.congress.gov/amendment-22. "No person shall be elected to the office of the President more than twice, ..."

39 https://www.cnn.com. "Trump admits he delayed Ukraine aid ..."President Donald Trump admitted Monday that he delayed aid to Ukraine ahead of a call to Ukrainian President Volodymyr Zelensky . . ." Written by Betsy Klein, September 24, 2019.

40 https://www.nytimes.com. "Ohio House Republican, "Calling Trump 'a Cancer,' Bows Out of 2022." Written by Jonathan Martin, September 16, 2021.

41 Indy Star, Opinion Op-ed: "Trump fired Coats for telling the truth. Trump's silencing the intelligence community is effectively turning the intelligence community into a group of yes men that will ignore the Russian threat ..." Written by Robert Weiner and Wes H. Cooper, September 22, 2019.

42 New York Times, "Trump, NBC Split $4.7 Million on Russian-Financed Miss Universe Pageant held in Moscow." Written by Jeremy Fuster, September 27, 2020.

43 https;//en.wikipedia.org. Aras Iskanderovich Agalarov is an Azerbaijani-Russian billionaire real estate developer. He is considered to be a Russian oligarch.

44 https://www.heritage.org. "8 Cities That Help Explain National Crime Wave. "The rise in violent crime has become a national trend in the past few years (under Trump's presidency) as cities reach homicide rates not seen in decades." Written by Jarrett Stepman, January 27, 2022

45 https://www.npr.org, "Trump, While Attacking Mail Voting, Casts Mail Ballot Again," August 19, 2020.

46 https://en.wikipedia.org/wiki/The_Holocaust.

47 https://www.express.co.uo, "Putin's stark similarities to Stalin laid bare – 5 key connections." Written by James Gray, May 18, 2022.

48 https://coronavirus.jhu.edu. "Experts say the tragic milestone likely occurred months ago; higher vaccinations could have prevent fatalities. The United States officially surpassed one million reported COVID-19 deaths on May 17, 2022, according to data from the John Hopkins Coronavirus Resource Center. Written by Doug Donovan.

Chapter Six

The Weight Of A Badge

Police psychology, also referred to as "police and public safety psychology," was formally recognized in 2013 by the American Psychological Association as a specialty in professional psychology.[1] They have no authority over police departments but work as consultants to improve police-community relations and to ensure law enforcement individuals are able to perform their jobs safely, effectively, ethically, and lawfully.

"Daniel Trummer[2] was 14 and Black, on the bus home from school in Frankfurt, Germany, when he noticed the frail-looking woman mumbling something in his direction that sounded like a racial epithet. She proceeded to unload on him by telling him to go home. Trummer was furious. If a classmate hadn't pulled him away, he's not sure what would have happened. It wasn't the last time Trummer, now a 35-year-old Portland (Oregon) police officer, experienced racism in his native Germany or in the U.S. after he immigrated. As far as racism, "it's a contributing factor because some White officers in Black neighborhoods see similar behaviors over and over again," he says. "So certain stereotypes get reinforced, and you create a bias towards a certain demographic... There's systemic racism in this country, for sure, because this country was built when Black lives didn't mean anything. They were animals, right? So if you continue building a country with that mindset, you're not going to prioritize those folks. In that sense, I really do support reform." Daniel Trummer is one of the "good cops" who wish to stay in law enforcement and help the system change from within.

Another police officer from Florida is Aaron Walp. He was an officer for thirty-one years. He said, "Putting on the badge in the morning changes your entire demeanor. You feel like a target because there are others who just may wish to kill you." In our interview [3] he recalled brutal fights where he thought the other guy would win – then backup arrived to help. He spoke about how it felt to think "the other man is going to murder you and dismember you – the reality is that when you go out on the streets, you are going to war and that only one of 300 officers last five years or more on the force." This lifestyle changed him. Certain attacks and fights left him reliving survival modes while seeing the horror of unspeakable crimes left long-lasting recurring nightmares. In one incident, he was beaten so severely that his sister did not recognize him. He did say, however, that racism never was a factor. Everyone in his unit hated the "bad cops." As a police officer, his job and that of others was to "uphold the law no matter what." However, the law itself is often crazy. In one situation, he crushed up seized marijuana and buried it in the dirt so it was unusable, then told the young offender to remember this if he wanted to stay out of jail. He calls this a tale about "chewing green."

Aaron Walp's story has a remarkable twist. Around the age of 29, he began to feel a calling to work with children and with God. After many years of studying theology and education, he earned a Ph.D. and is now the Head Administrator of a Christian elementary school. This position gives him an opportunity to help guide youth away from making the mistakes that would eventually land them in jail or even prison. His philosophy is that this work provides youngsters the decision-making skills to make the right choices in life. While he says he loved police work and occasionally struggles with not going back, he feels the role he plays today is just as, or more important – working with youth and preventing potential future crime. [31]

The following brief article was published in *The Washington Post*[4] in June 2020. It's called "Black Officers, torn between badge and culture, face uniquely painful questions." [32]

Sweat pooled under Khaled Abdelghany's National Guard helmet on a hot day in May outside of the nation's capital. The 32-year-old soldier stood scanning the crowd, reading the handwritten signs decrying police brutality and racial injustice.

If he was honest, he didn't want to be there — or, at least, he didn't want to be on the law enforcement side. Because as a Black man, he supported the demonstrations. And as he stood there, he thought he could have been George Floyd, the man whose death in police custody set off this historic wave of dissent. That's what was on his mind when the protesters started a chant: "I'm Black and I'm proud."

Abdelghany joined in, mouthing the words. The moment, captured in an 18-second video and shared widely online, was a powerful symbol of a conflict felt by many people of color sent to the front lines of America's protests in recent months.

On another sizzling summer day, Michelle Bracken, national president for the National Organization of Black Women in Law Enforcement and an inspector at a federal agency, heard all-too-familiar phrases such as "Uncle Tom," "sellout," or "traitor" hurled her way as she surveilled protests and protected monuments emblematic of America's promise and a president who has been accused of thwarting it for Black citizens.

Bracken's years of workplace racial and gender harassment steeled her, making her impenetrable to insults and thrown rocks any wayward person in a crowd could muster. Her faith in God and her commitment to her job in law enforcement for 31 years outweighed any personal turmoil over the duality of being Black and in uniform.

"They've got a whole lot of good names out there for you," she said. "As an individual, I have to be grounded, because I'm not that. I'm here to protect and to serve."

Officers like Abdelghany and Bracken wear the uniform of the police or military, and yet they have experienced some of the same unequal treatment the demonstrators are voicing. They feel torn between a professional duty to carry out orders and a personal stake in changing the way Black Americans are treated. At the same time, some have faced protesters' ire, the recipients of painful insults of which only they could be the target, for their perceived role in upholding unjust systems and insults."

Despite the "good cops" – and <u>there are many</u>, statistics prove that there are also a large number of police officers across our country who are wearing badges but do not understand the difference between their job descriptions and unnecessary violence or even brutality. Most days, they look and behave like their fellow officers. The crimes these officers commit are lethal, and many go unreported.

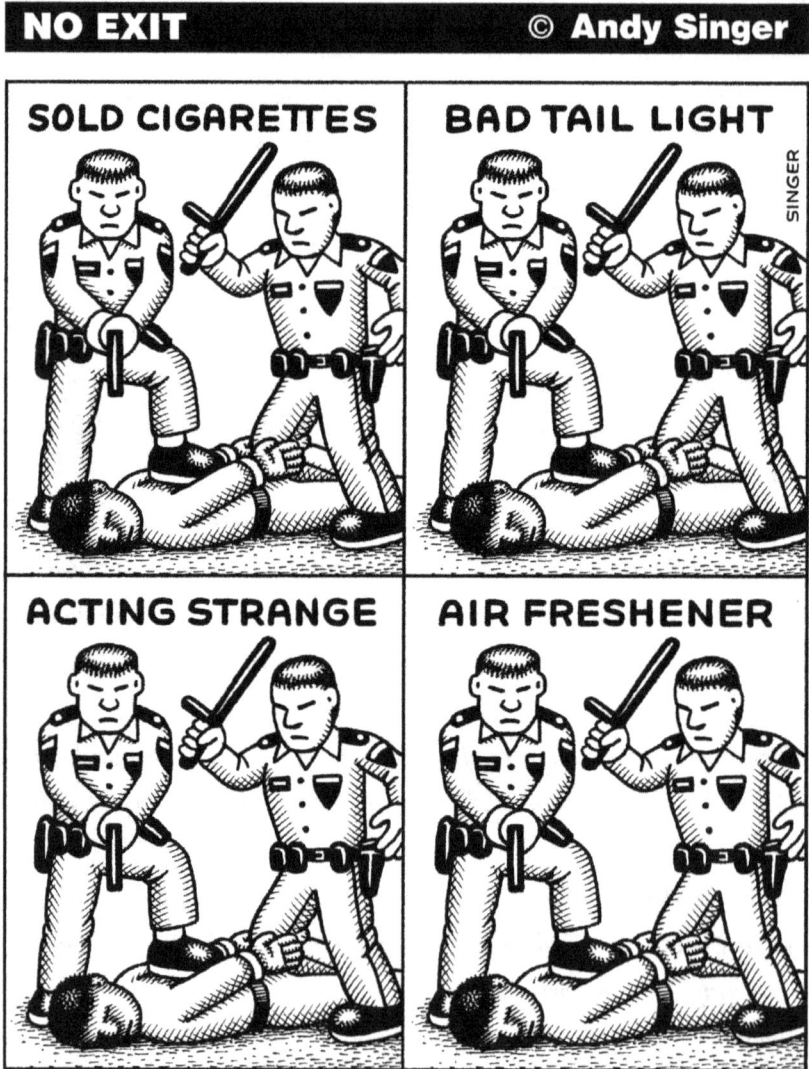

"Police Killings," Artist – Andy Singer, Courtesy of Cagle Cartoons.

Police Brutality in the United States[5]

If you have any doubt about the vast and extensive reality of police brutality or extensive racism in the United States, the following is a list of twenty-seven states and specific events that happened in those states. The names of these victims have been underlined.

These are all pulled from the FBI Crime Database. There are countless others which are not mentioned, and the number of incidents have escalated over the last twenty years.

Arizona

In November 2011, Police Officer Richard Chrisman in Phoenix responded to a domestic disturbance call at the home of <u>Danny Rodriguez</u>. Danny was twenty-eight years old at the time. When Danny picked up a bicycle in the living room, the officer shot him twice and then shot and killed his dog. The officer was charged with second-degree murder, aggravated assault, and animal cruelty. Two years later, Officer Chrisman was convicted and sentenced to seven years in prison.

California

California has a long list of cases concerning police brutality, beginning in 1951 when approximately fifty police officers participated in beating seven Latino men.

In 2014, a California Highway Patrol officer repeatedly punched <u>Marlene Pinnock</u>, a fifty-one-year-old bipolar woman, near the side of a freeway in Los Angeles. The officer, Daniel Andrew, resigned from the Highway Patrol and criminal charges against him are still pending.

In June and July 2000, the Oakland Police Department, known as the "Oakland Riders," were accused of violations of civil rights, unlawful beatings, and unlawful detentions by 119 citizens.

In July 2002, a tourist videotaped the beating of a sixteen-year-old named <u>Donovan Jackson</u> by the Inglewood Police. The video shows the officer repeatedly punching Jackson.

In July, 2011 a thirty-seven-year-old homeless man who was suffering from schizophrenia was fatally beaten by several members of the Fullerton Police. He was unarmed and mentally ill. An account of this incident says that he was beaten with flashlights and shocked with Tasers by up to six police officers.

In April 2014, Police Officer Sergio Alvarez was sentenced to 205 years on eighteen counts of sexually assaulting women and kidnapping while working the "graveyard shift" with the West Sacramento Police Department.

Among the more famous California cases was the Rodney King arrest and beating in 1991. This incident was video-taped by a bystander. Four police officers were charged with assault and other crimes but were acquitted. Their acquittals led to the 1992 Los Angeles riots, which were watched not only across the U.S. but around the world.

At the time, I was in Moscow watching the Rodney King beatings and feeling ashamed of the police in the U.S. My Russian friends flooded me with questions about police brutality in the U.S.

Colorado

The state of Colorado also has a long list of police infractions.

In January 2009, Alexander Landau and Addison Hunold were driving when they were pulled over for an illegal left turn. The officer asked for consent to perform a vehicle search, and when Landau requested to see a search warrant, the officer, along with two others, responded by punching him in the face, knocking him down, and beating him. Landau heard one of the officers say, "Where is that warrant now you fucking nigger?"

In July 2010, the use of force by Denver Police Officers resulted in the death of Marvin Booker.

Connecticut

In December 1998, Franklin Reid, a nineteen-year-old, was shot and killed during a foot chase. Officer Scott Smith was tried and appealed his case and pleaded no contest to misdemeanor criminally negligent homicide. His sentence was two years of probation.

Florida

"On the night of February 26, 2012, in Sanford, Florida, United States, George Zimmerman fatally shot Trayvon Martin, a seventeen-year-old African-American high school student. At the time of the shooting, Zimmerman, a twenty-eight-year-old man of mixed race, was the neighborhood watch coordinator for his gated community where Martin was visiting relatives. Treyvon was walking back to his relatives' house after buying goods at a local store. Zimmerman shot Martin, who was unarmed, without any provocation." Zimmerman was tried and was acquitted. Protests erupted across the U.S. and the phrase "Black Lives Matter" was born.

On June 24, 2015, at Pinewood, Florida (north of Miami), King Carter was shot and killed. He was only six-years-old.

Georgia

On November 21, 2006, police officers entered a home with a "no-knock" warrant that was based on false information. The resident was a ninety-two-year-old Atlanta woman who was shot and killed. The police planted false evidence but were eventually convicted of manslaughter.

Illinois

Illinois is a state that has multiple incidents that demonstrate police brutality.

In October 2009, a fifteen-year-old Marshawn Pitts was beaten by Dolton police officer Christopher Lloyd at a school for special needs children. This beating was recorded on surveillance cameras.

In June 2011, police responded to a domestic disturbance allegedly involving Flint Farmer. Farmer fled the scene and was shot multiple times by the police. The video shows that he was shot in the leg, in the abdomen, and several times in the back, while on the ground.

Iowa

In Kellogg, Iowa, in September 2020, four people were charged in the strangulation death and burning of Michael Williams, a forty-four-year-old Black man.

Kentucky

On March 13, 2020, Breona Taylor, a Black woman, was shot and killed by police in Louisville. She was in her own home, in bed, at the time, and completely innocent of any crime.

Louisiana

In March 1990, <u>Adolph Archie</u>, who is a Black man, killed a White police officer. Moments later, a security guard shot Archie in the arm and he was placed in a patrol car for transport to the hospital. The police radio was on and witnesses heard the police officers talking about killing Archie. Officers arrived at the hospital, but for some reason, Archie never made it into the hospital. Instead, he was taken to the precinct of the officer who he killed and was beaten to death there.

In September 2005, <u>Henry Glover</u> was shot, killed, and then burned by New Orleans police officers. Glover had been near a mall and was mistaken for a looter.

In September 2005, after Hurricane Katrina, a shooting occurred on the Danziger Bridge in New Orleans. Seventeen-year-old <u>James Brissette</u> and forty-year-old <u>Ronald Madison</u> were killed, and four other civilians were wounded. All of the victims were unarmed. Madison, who was a mentally disabled man, was shot in the back. The New Orleans police then created a cover-up story attempting to say that the civilians were armed. New Orleans Federal Court found five of the police officers guilty of a list of charges.

Maryland

In June 2008, a U.S. Marine was fatally shot by an off-duty Baltimore police officer. It was reported that Mr. <u>Brown</u> had made an advance toward the police officer's girlfriend. Several witnesses said that Brown was turning to leave when the police officer shot him.

In September 2012, a police officer from District Heights pulled over <u>Calvin Kyle</u> on suspicion of driving a stolen motorcycle. The police officer shot Kyle while he was handcuffed, which left Kyle paralyzed from the waist down.

Michigan

In November 1992, <u>Malice Green</u> died while in police custody. He had been arrested during a routine traffic stop. Green was struck in the head with a flashlight approximately fourteen times, which caused his death.

Minnesota

On April 2, 2005, a suspect was handcuffed, pepper-sprayed in his eyes and nostrils, and then arrested for bank robbery. A review of the 911 transcript clearly revealed that the Golden Valley police had twice been told that a White male in a white van had robbed the local bank. Mr. Hixon, the man arrested and pepper-sprayed, was a dark-skinned Black man who was refueling his Jaguar.

On May 25, 2020, George Floyd, a forty-six-year-old Black man, was killed by Minneapolis police while being arrested on suspicion of using a twenty-dollar counterfeit bill.

February 26, 2021, Daunte Wright, a twenty-year-old Black man, was shot and killed by police in Brooklyn Center. The female police officer who shot him said it was a "mistake." She has been charged with manslaughter.

Mississippi

In May 1970, the police attempted to break up a crowd of about 100 Black students protesting near Jackson State University. In the process, they shot and killed two Black students and injured twelve others.

In February 2006, Jessie Lee Williams Jr. was beaten by a police jailer and later died of his injuries.

Missouri

The police of Kansas City pulled over a Sudanese native who was having a miscarriage and was on her way to the hospital. This woman pleaded with the officers to let her go to the hospital, but one officer was heard saying, "How's that my problem?" They took her to jail, where she delivered her baby who lived for only one minute.

In August 2014, Michael Brown Jr., an eighteen-year-old Black man, was fatally shot by a White police officer in Ferguson, Missouri. Protesters who witnessed the shooting said that Michael had his hands up and said, "don't shoot."

Nevada

In 2011, a Las Vegas police officer shot and killed an unarmed man. This officer, Jesus Arevalo, was fired but not convicted of a crime.

In 2013, another Las Vegas police officer sexually assaulted two women in separate incidents. He was only sentenced to two years in prison. Typically, a charge of sexual assault results in a ten-year prison sentence.

New Jersey

In May 2009, a police officer was video recorded by a surveillance camera hitting a forty-nine-year-old schizophrenic with his fists and a baton. He was suspended.

New Mexico

Stephen Silvin was arrested in August 2005 and charged with driving while intoxicated and with a stolen vehicle. He was in jail for twenty-two months before going to trial, at which time the judge declared him incompetent and dismissed all charges. Silvin claimed that he requested medical attention multiple times but was denied care.

New York

In April 1985, NYPD detectives arrested Mark Davidson on charges of selling marijuana. He was then booked at the 106th Precinct in Queens, where he was tortured with a stun gun and threatened with the same painful torture on his genitals.

In July 1996, a New York City Police officer shot in the back Nathaniel Levi Gaines. Gaines was unarmed and waiting for the Southbound D train at 167th Street.

In August 1997, while detained in a New York City police station, Abner Louima was sodomized with a broken broomstick. He was left bleeding from the rectum in a booking cell.

In February 1999, four New York City police officers shot forty-one times, killing unarmed Amadou Diallo.

In May 2003, a plainclothes New York City police officer shot Ousmane Zongo to death. He was suspected of being involved with a CD theft group but was found to be innocent.

In November 2006, three men were shot a total of fifty times by a team of NYPD officers. Sean Bell was killed in this incident the day after his bachelor party. Two of his friends were wounded.

In July 2014, at Staten Island, New York, the world watched as Eric Garner was suffocated and killed by the police. One officer was fired, but he never faced criminal charges.

Oklahoma

In a bizarre incident in May 2010, an emergency medical technician (EMT) was assaulted by Oklahoma Highway Patrol Officer. The dash camera video told the entire story. The ambulance was pulled over for failing to yield, even though there was a patient in the back who needed to reach the hospital quickly. The officer then tried to arrest the EMT and used a chokehold. Another officer intervened and eventually the EMT was allowed to take his patient to the hospital.

Ohio

In January 2008, SWAT officers raided the home of Tarika Wilson and her six children. They had an arrest warrant for her boyfriend, who was allegedly a drug dealer. Tarika was fatally shot, and her one-year-old son was wounded.

Oregon

In May 2003, Kendra James was a passenger in a car that was stopped by Portland Police. She was twenty-one years old. After the driver was subdued and removed from the car, James tried to escape in the car since there was a warrant for her arrest. The police randomly shot then claimed that they did not know that she was hit. James died four hours later.

Pennsylvania

In 1988, a Philadelphia police officer beat Tracy McDaniel.

In 1990, also in Philadelphia, the police beat David Hayes with nightsticks, causing him permanent brain damage.

In 1995, six Philadelphia police officers were arrested for robbing and assaulting forty Black people. This was known as the "39th District Corruption Scandal" and was publicized worldwide.

In 2003, a Philadelphia police officer was convicted of sexually assaulting a thirteen-year-old girl multiple times while on duty.

In 2007, another Philadelphia officer fatally shot mental patient Reora Askew five times, including twice in the back.

In 2008, three compliant Black men were beaten by several Philadelphia officers during a routine traffic stop. This incident was videotaped.

In 2010, another Philadelphia police officer was charged and convicted for sexual assault on a prisoner.

South Carolina

In February 1968, nine South Carolina Highway Patrol Officers in Orangeburg shot into an unarmed group of protestors. Their shots hit most of the victims in the back. Three men were killed and twenty-eight more injured. Other protestors were beaten and injured by the police, including one pregnant woman who later had a miscarriage.

In November 2003, the police staged a raid at Stratford High School at gunpoint and forced students as young as fourteen to lay on the ground while the police and dogs searched schoolbags.

Texas

In May 1977, six police officers arrested a twenty-three-year-old Vietnam War Vet for disorderly conduct. The officers took him to a place called Buffalo Bayou and beat him, then shoved him into the water. His body was found several days later.

Washington State

In May 2006, a young Black man was beaten to death by Spokane police. He had been falsely accused of stealing from an ATM.

Wisconsin

In October 2004, three off-duty Milwaukee police officers attended a house party where Frank Jude, Jr. was beaten. He was unarmed. Several other officers also took part in the beating.

In August 2020, Jacob Blake was shot seven times in the back by police in Kenosha. He is now paralyzed.

This is a short list of police brutality recorded throughout the U.S. Typically, police officers serve little time in prison for serious crimes compared to others committing similar crimes. For example, sexual assault or rape convictions usually result in a minimum ten-year sentence, but if committed by a police officer, the sentence typically is probation or two years. [6]

There are an average of ten murders a day in a population of less than seven million in El Salvador. Guatemala and other countries in Central America. [7]Immigrants, believing that the U.S. is less violent and evil, walk more than 2,000 miles to reach the "land of their dreams." Full of optimism and hope, these people search for a better life and their bodies are fueled by endorphins rather than food. They have no idea what obstacles they will face once reaching the U.S. border.

No one tells them that the U.S. is riddled with hatred for Blacks and immigrants or that our police may "shoot to kill." According to a recent *New York Times* article, [8] "approximately thirty-two Latinos and Hispanics will die within any twenty-day period at the hands of U.S. police officers."

For immigrants, the reality between a "land of dreams" and real-life U.S. police daily operations is vast. This gap is even larger for other minorities in the U.S.

Black citizens in the US risk their lives every time they leave their homes.

CHAPTER 6 – END NOTES

1 https://concept.paloaltou.edu. "What is Police Psychology . . ." CONCEPT, Palo Alto University.

2 https://people.com, "How a Black Portland Cop Hopes to 'Effect Internal Change'," Written by Winston Ross, October 29, 2020.

3 Interview between the author and Aaron Walp, Ph.D., October 13, 2020.

4 The Washington Post, "Black Officers torn between badge and culture, face uniquely painful questons," Written by Lateshn Beachum and Brittany Shammas, June 2020.

5 All information in this Chapter was gleaned from the FBI crime database. As of September 30, 2021, the FBI reported that Police murders of Blacks in the U.S. are under-reported by 50%.

6 As the Executive Director of the Arizona Sexual Assault Network funded by the U.S. Department of Justice, I conducted two years of research inside a sex-offender prison and studied sex abuse, assault, and laws.

7 https://worldpopulationreview.com, "Murder Rate by Country 2021."

8 https://www.nytimes.com, "Death on the Border: Were Two Brothers Hunting Migrants or Wildlife?" Written by JMES Dobbins, J. David Goodman, and Edgar Sandoval, October 12, 2022

Chapter Seven

Healing

So what do you plan to do now? You have heard the evidence. You have
seen the videos and the news clippings. You watched George Floyd die on
the evening news. For more than nine minutes, Officer Chauvin sat on his neck
while listening to George plead for his life.[1] The proof of second-degree murder is
indisputable, and this unprovoked killing and brutality by four members of our
law enforcement is just one example of police officers believing they can act with
impunity or that they will not be held accountable for brutality or even murder.

If you deny this distorted reality of our democracy, then you are fooling no one
but yourselves. Derek Chauvin, the officer who knelt on George Floyd's neck,
was tried and found guilty of murder.[2] Justice prevailed in this case, but there are
hundreds more cases not even investigated, as well as other crimes that have been
covered up or ignored.

"What about Unity?" Artist – John Darkow, Courtesy of Cagle Cartoons.

A front-page article in the *New York Times* on Sunday, June 7, 2020 states: "Over the past five years, as demands for reform have mounted in the aftermath of police violence in cities like Ferguson, MO., police unions have emerged as one of the most significant roadblocks to change. The greater the political pressure for reform, the more defiant the unions often are in resisting it – with few city officials, including liberal leaders, able to overcome their opposition."[3] Perhaps the police unions are a starting point for police behavior change?

"In the wake of George Floyd's killing by now-former Minneapolis Police Department officer Derek Chauvin, few have been inclined to defend Chauvin or his colleagues who stood by and watched as he suffocated Floyd to death. Few, that is, except Bob Kroll.

In a letter to membership, Kroll – the president of the MPD's police union – referred to protesters outraged by police brutality as a "terrorist movement" and defended the officers who killed Floyd and were subsequently fired, arguing they were "terminated without due process" and lamenting, "What is not being told is the violent criminal history of George Floyd." (Truth – Floyd had a criminal record, but mostly for nonviolent drug and theft charges.)

Kroll's statements illustrate a central challenge in American efforts to transform policing: Police unions, the groups that represent police officers, are a powerful force that stands in the way of holding police accountable. Minneapolis Mayor Jacob Frey told the New York Times that Kroll and his union are a major reason it's hard to bring order to the Minneapolis Police Department, saying they create a "nearly impenetrable barrier" to reform.

In Buffalo, the city's Police Benevolent Association president John Evans has actively defended officers who pushed seventy-five-year-old White demonstrator Martin Gugino to the ground. (Note: he was left bleeding and then hospitalized). When the officers who pushed Gugino were seen leaving their arraignment on felony assault charges, a large crowd of police union members and sympathizers was seen cheering them on. In New York State, police unions led opposition to newly signed legislation that prevents police from hiding misconduct complaints and criminalizes chokeholds.

The foregrounding of police unions' role in the warping of American law enforcement has also prompted some difficult conversations on the left. The presence of a segment of a union movement that's unapologetically right-wing and hostile to Black communities has tested the limits of solidarity from more left-wing unionists.

As long as police forces exist, police unions will exist in some form as well, even if just as political pressure groups. It is therefore natural to think that reforming police unions in some way must be part of the broader agenda of changing policing in America. They are among the biggest stakeholders in the way the system works now; without addressing their power, other reforms may never get off the ground."

How do we "police" the police and the police unions?

Every one of us who lives in the United States needs to heal. It would be challenging to believe that anyone who viewed George Floyd die on live TV was not affected somehow. Many of us became angry to the point of action. Some of us openly cried. And others, especially those demonstrators in the streets allowed their emotions to be seen and felt. There were some Americans who felt numb. They have become complacent to the many demonstrations, riots, and political issues seen on the nightly news. And yes, other rioters were looting and setting fire to buildings and cars. These opportunists were self-focused and not concerned with the more significant issues of police brutality or the murder of Blacks on city streets across the United States.

The term "civil society" was devised decades ago and means "the space for collective action around shared interests, purposes and values, generally distinct from government and commercial for-profit actors." [4] It is about inclusion, public communications, reciprocity of tolerance, patience, and the overall good of society. Since the death of George Floyd, the collective action across our country has been mass demonstrations denouncing the police brutality that led to his death. There has been an awakening – but then again, how could his death and his plea for his life be inferred as anything but a revival? Both Blacks and Whites have recognized the injustice of his death. The historical collective grievances of victimized minority communities were expressed day after day in large and small cities across our nation as well as around the globe.

It's also impossible not to compare the death of George Floyd to that of Jesus Christ. Jesus pleaded with God the Father to spare his life, but his death on the cross has become an instrumental guiding light to teach humanity the differences between a righteous life and one filled with hatred and murder. George did not die in vain, as thousands of people recognized the evil actions resulting in his human sacrifice. His spirit and soul will live on and hopefully will change the revulsion and the brutality of our police and others whose brains are responding to the chemistry of hatred.

In the book *White Fragility*, the Conclusions, Robin DiAngelo wrote:

"The default of the current system is the reproduction of racial inequality; our institutions were designed to reproduce racial inequality and they do so with efficiency. Our schools are particularly effective at this task. To continue reproducing racial inequality, the system only needs White people to be really nice and carry on, smile at people of color, be friendly across race, and go to lunch together on occasion. I am not saying that you shouldn't be nice. I suppose it's better than being mean. But niceness is not courageous. Niceness will not get racism on the table and will not keep it on the table when everyone wants it off. In fact, bringing racism to White people's attention is often seen as NOT nice, and being perceived as not nice triggers White fragility."

If George Floyd's spirit is to live on in the hearts of Americans, we need to consciously fight the current atmosphere of hatred that permeates so many American souls. I would imagine that many readers – especially those who are White – may feel uneasy and apprehensive reading this book or some of the other books that I have recommended, but it's a first step.

As a second step, become involved. Ask what you can do to change your thoughts and your life, your neighborhood, your community, your city, and our nation. Be informed and open the conversation about racism and the benefits of diversity. Be a part of the solution and not a part of the "closed-minded" group spreading further hatred that too often results in more violence.

Created initially as an interfaith nonprofit organization, the Institute of Cultural Affairs (ICA)[5] in Chicago was founded with a mission to "help individuals, families, organizations, and communities work together to build hopeful, just, and sustainable societies." ICA teaches participatory methods of strategic planning, problem-solving, and conflict resolution that generate ownership in organizational, corporate, or government change. Founded about fifty years ago, this organization originated/established the profession of facilitation. They have affiliate offices and representatives across the U.S. and the globe, and some divisions offer diversity training. They may be able to be of assistance to you or your community – together, create the change you wish to see in your town or in your own life!

Another excellent book to acquire and read is *The Change Handbook, Group Methods for Shaping the Future.* This book was authored by members of the Institute of Cultural Affairs and is an appeal to implement change in the U.S. toward a more just society and to fulfill the ideal stated by our founding fathers that "all men are created equal."

While these resources may help, our government and our country's leadership needs to send social marketing messages[6] using TV, social media, the internet, and all other sources to preach nonviolence. President Biden, President Obama, President Bush, must be the message senders. Social marketing messages must be reiterated often in order to show results and they must out-shine the negative, hateful messages sent by Trump or his loyalists via social media.

Just about everyone in this country loves football. It's a game where anyone can support their hometown team, sit at home, eat popcorn and hot dogs, and cheer for their boys to win. As the NFL has gone from only one or two Black players in the 1920s to the year 2020, where the majority of the players are Black[7], race has not mattered to the fans. We still cheer for our teams no matter what. For a short period of time – the length of four 15-minute quarters of play – RACE does not matter.

As the Chief Operating Officer of a small company in Phoenix, Arizona, I used to have staff meetings where I often compared the company to a football team. The team had a common goal – to help build the company and sell its products. The group supported each other in all efforts. We hugged, we jumped up and down and even danced in celebration over "wins" or "touchdowns." Big orders required that we order pizza. We consoled each other if we lost an order because we were a cohesive team. We stuck together through thick and thin, good and bad. We won some games and lost others, but we always maintained our "football team" spirit.

Well, folks – we are all Americans and we are all on the same team. When you feel that nasty urge to be discriminate against others, STOP. Think about your favorite football team and remember cheering them on. It felt positive and inclusive. Discrimination and racism are about hate. You have a choice about how you wish to feel – and you know the exhilaration of being on a team or cheering for your team where the color of a person's skin is not important. Go back to that place in your mind and relive it anytime you wish. It is also a far more healthy way to live.

Last, when I was in college in California during the late 1960s, I lived in the dorms. My Jewish roommate was from New York and we often discussed racial inequality. The following is a short story that I wrote for a college course. The assignment was to write a one-page story to help people empathize with others and to better comprehend the idiocy and absurdity of prejudice and racial hatred. I got an A- on this story.

Today is my birthday and I will be eleven years old. I am excited and will be having several friends from my school come to my house for a small birthday party. Two of my friends are Black, one is Hispanic, one is White, and two are Jewish, as is my family. Everyone is having a great time and my mother brought out a beautiful chocolate cake that she made just for my birthday. Everyone sang Happy Birthday to me and my mother lit the candles. I got the first piece of cake and it was delicious. Half my face was covered in chocolate icing.

There was a knock on the door. Thinking that this is someone wishing me a happy birthday, I opened it. In walked three Hispanic-looking men with guns. They ask if anyone there is Jewish. My mother spoke with the men and asked them why they wanted to know? They answered her by saying "unless someone points out the Jewish children, we will take all of the children with us as well as the parents." Since no one dared say anything, the men forcefully pushed my parents and all my friends into a black unmarked van with no windows. My parents tried to comfort all of us, but the smell of mortal fear penetrated our clothes. I was so scared that I almost threw up my birthday cake.

We drove for several hours in this van until we reached an army-type of camp outside of the city. My mother and father were separated into different camps and my friends and I drove for another hour to a different place.

Once we arrived at the camp, myself and three other friends went to one building and my Black and Hispanic friends were sent elsewhere. We were not fed much and were given old dirty clothes to wear. There was only one shower for maybe fifty kids and the building smelled like a dirty barn. The cots were uncomfortable, and each of us received one unwashed blanket and pillow.

The next day, the boys were forced to work in the fields for long hours. Another girl and I were photographed nude in various embarrassing positions that made me feel uncomfortable and truly scared. I screamed when I was told later that we would be trafficked as sex slaves for other soldiers. I understood what this meant, but my friend did not. She was only ten years old. No one knew what happened to my parents, but I never saw them again.

The Black and Hispanic children were driven back to the city. Their parents were so relieved to see them returned and unharmed. After I was released many years later, I learned that these "friends from school" were told that in the future, they should never befriend a White person or a Jewish person. That these White people are an inferior race; they lack an essential human heredity gene; and that is why their skin has no color.

> **The reality is that human differences between races, religions, or tribes are superficial and hating anyone who does not resemble YOU is ludicrous.**

Do you really want hatred to consume you and destroy your life? Do you really want domestic terrorists – fueled by senseless and mindless rage - to obliterate your government buildings, your house of worship, your small business, or your own home? These messages and speeches containing hatred toward others came from Trump and have been proved to be forms of brain-washing.

Do you want to go out to buy groceries and risk being shot and killed by local police officers? Well America, this is exactly what happens in our country. Every time a Black teen runs to the store to buy milk – their mother or father worries that they may be killed.

ALL PARENTS IN THE U.S. SHOULD ASK THEMSELVES TO IMAG-
INE LIVING WITH THE DAILY FEAR OF VIOLENTLY LOSING THEIR
CHILD TO SENSELESS POLICE VIOLENCE, BRUTALITY, RACISM,
AND MURDER.

I know the agony of losing a child. It is a throbbing grief that consumes a parent
every minute of their life thereafter.

As my father said to me many times as a child –

> **"You are no better or worse than anyone else in this world."**

CHAPTER 7 – END NOTES

1 https://www.cnn.com. "Former officer knelt on George Floyd for 9 minutes and 29 seconds." Written by Eric Levenson, March 30, 2021.

2 https:www.cnn.com, "Derek Chauvin found guilty of all three charges for killing George Floyd," Written by Eirc Levenson and Aaron Cooper, April 21, 2021.

3 https://www.nytimes.com, "How Police Unions Became Such Powerful Opponents to Reform Efforts.", Written by Noami Scheiber, Farah Stockman and J. David Goodman, April 2, 2021.

4 https://www.forum.org, "Who and what is 'civil society?', A World Economic Forum." Written by Adam Jezard, April 23, 2018.

5 https://www.ica-usa.org, ICA's website says: "Release the capacity to create positive, sustainable futures."

6 https://www/frpg-dog.com, "What is a social marketing message? Similar to selling a product or service, social marketing uses commercial marketing techniques to promote the adoption of behaviors that will improve health or well-being of a specific target audience. Communities, conversations, channels and campaigns that drive word-of-mouth buzz are the 4C's of social media marketing."

7 https://en.wikipedia.org. "Fritz Pollard and Bobby Marshall were the first Black players in what is now the NFL in 1920. Pollard became the first (and until 1989, the only) Black coach in 1921."

Chapter Eight

What To Believe

J oe South sang "Games People Play" many decades ago.[1] The words are still true today. This song also reminds me of a line in the 1990's movie called *Russia House.*[2] In short, Sean Connery played "Boozy" Bartholomew (Barley) Scott Blair, a British book store owner. Michelle Pfeiffer played Katya Orlova, a beautiful Russian book publisher. "Katya attempts to pass Barley a manuscript, but it is not any usual book – it purports to contain the truth about Soviet nuclear capabilities. The manuscript goes astray and ends up in the hands of British Intelligence, who then also confer with the CIA."[3] In one scene, the CIA, the British Intelligence, and Barley are holed up in an expansive mansion on a Swiss mountain lake to determine if Barley is a spy or just caught up in a manuscript gone off course. One of the CIA agents asks Barley why he goes to Russia more than he comes to the U.S. Barley responds by stating: "Russia is just as corrupt as the U.S., but there is so much less bullshit in Russia."[4] I found this statement to be profoundly accurate.

Our country is so full of bull shit that people no longer know what to believe – especially about Trump. This results in people voting along party lines without a concerned conscience or a logical and informed decision process. Voting is not intended to be a rote process – it is a serious responsibility. It requires each voter to study their choices and vote based on factual information. Intelligent voting is critical to a democracy and should not be about "loyalty" to a party or a man.

This book does not intend to disparage democracy as a form of government. After traveling and experiencing the world, I chose to live in the United States because this is still home. However, by 2020, "democrazy" in the U.S. has strayed far from the course set by our Constitution and our Founding Fathers. The list of reasons include capitalism, racism and bigotry, economics, hatred and police brutality, isolation, and a two-party form of government – where one party chooses to believe and spread lies, or simply doesn't know the difference, or they have been unknowingly brain-washed. Other issues faced by our democracy includes widespread and massive infiltration, misinformation, and strategic disinformation from outside sources such as Russia and China.

In addition, recent damage to the U.S. economy is voluminous.

> **In the second quarter of 2020, the US economy dropped 32.9%.**

5

This was the largest descent in the history of the United States. And yes, Trump was accountable for this fiscal blunder because managing the U.S. economy is included in the job description handed to every single President of the United States. "Donald Trump built a national debt so big (even before the pandemic) that it will weight down our country's economy for years."[6]

As a reminder, Trump has declared bankruptcy four times – not just once! Once is a mistake, but four bankruptcies are an indication of gross financial mismanagement or deliberate fraud. Do you really trust Trump with your hard-earned income and the federal taxes that you have paid?

Capitalism – In less than a century, our country has transformed into one where people will do just about anything for money. The growing inequality of those who have wealth and those who do not has split our society in two. This disparity has also creeped into government, where each department of the federal or state governments fight and distort reality to increase budgets unnecessarily. The Department of Corrections fills prison beds to justify a larger budget. Every single department of government in Washington, D.C. needs to cut their budgets by 10% to 20%.

Racism – Racism has been the evil force that initiated many wars in countries around the world, but the U.S. form of racism is distinct, conspicuous, and undeniable. The reason our form of bias is unique is that it is based on a contradiction – a big fat lie. The United States was founded on the premise that all men are created equal, yet the founding fathers treated slaves – who were just as human as the slave owners – as animals. This dichotomy is one reason why other countries around the world no longer believe in our democracy. The George Floyd murder and many others are evidence that not much has changed in hundreds of years.

> **We cannot call ourselves the "land of the free", when we murder our own citizens due to the color of their skin.**

Economics – As mentioned in the Preface, here are the facts regarding our economy:

In 2020, the U.S. trade balance was a negative $676.7 billion[7]. Economists use the trade balance of a country to measure the country's economic stability.

Our government regularly increases our debt ceiling – allowing our debt to accumulate at an extremely high interest rate, instead of decreasing spending.

Forty-one percent of the U.S. trade deficit in goods is with China, a communist country. China is now hoarding food supplies and storing it instead of trading it.

In 2019, U.S. Government spending was up 49.1% from the previous year, while income was down 13.4%. This was before the COVID-19 virus arrived in the U.S. in January 2020. This drastic increase in spending was partially due to the taxpayers paying for Trump's lavish lifestyle and his twenty-seven visits to Mar-a-Largo at a cost of about $13 million for security alone. In addition, Trump spent close to $118 million in travel and security costs for more than 227 days at other various golf resorts that HE OWNS. A large portion of your tax money went directly into Trump's pocket and his businesses. The U.S. Constitution has a domestic emoluments clause, which forbids U.S. Presidents from accepting personal remunerations beyond their approved salary. Trump ignored this law. Putin is now one of the richest men in Europe, and he used his position as President to gain this wealth. Trump followed Putin's example.

> **Donald Trump put his personal interests above his sworn duty to our democracy - and to YOU, all citizens of the USA.**

In 2018, the Russian trade balance was positive $165.29 billion, they have a monopoly of the gas and oil for Europe, and they are debt free.

In 2018, China's trade balance was positive $106 billion.

Can the wealthy in the U.S. actually be taxed enough to pay off our debt, or would their expert tax preparers manipulate their tax returns so no tax would be paid?

Would major corporations agree to be taxed at 25% to 40%, or would they pack up and move to Mexico or to China to avoid this tax?

Our federal government needs to cut federal spending by 10% to 20% across all departments, balance our budget, stop creating and engaging in war, and not spend more than what is essential for government operations.

"Easter Bunny Economics," Artist – John Cole, Courtesy of Cagle Cartoons.

Hatred – In a country where hate festers and grows, society loses. Hatred in America has replaced moral upbringing, religious teachings, and basic human respect for our fellow citizens, our neighbors, and our families. Hate is evident in the two-party political system, in racial issues, and struggles between our police and our communities. It was a part of every speech given to the American public by President Trump. The FBI reported in their crime data base that:

> **In the year 2020, murders in the United States were up by 30% and there were more than 7,700 hate crimes.**

Trump's speeches filled with hatred encouraged others to commit violence and crimes.

Hate is destroying the very fabric of our ideals as a nation, as demonstrated by the domestic terrorists that vandalized and damaged the U.S. Capitol on January

6, 2021. Oxygenated by Trump, who was breastfed by Putin, this violent act was domestic terrorism. Hatred will bury all of us if it is allowed to continue. What more could Putin want?

Isolation – The majority of Americans never travel abroad, never learn other languages or understand other cultures, and never grasp that the U.S. is just one country among many on our mother earth.

Our country has two neighbors – Canada and Mexico. Trump alienated us from both (i.e., "who will pay for the border wall – Mexico"), from our free world partners in NATO, and just about all other nations. This is a top priority for Putin because he knows if the U.S. is isolated, it is more vulnerable.

Trump's policies increased U.S. isolation, especially concerning trade. President Biden needs to reverse this course if possible, but trade goes in two directions. The damage done by Trump may not easily be reversed if other world leaders are cautious about all forms of partnerships, especially international trade and military support, with the U.S. Who could blame them?

The United States is no longer the leader of the free world and we do not have the same level of international clout as before Trump. We are a country drowning in debt, irrational racism, police killing the very citizens they are hired to protect, violence around every corner, and the rich vs. poor – with little room in between. We are in trouble.

Inflation – Inflation in the United States as of November 2021, has impacted the approval rating of President Biden. Inflation prices of meat, gas and oil, other groceries and goods, are all due to Russia's cyber-attacks on the supply chain and delivery of products to the American consumer. Microsoft has proved that at least 58% of the supply chain issues in the U.S. are due to Russian hacking.[8] So blame Putin and not Biden for your higher prices at the pump or the grocery store. This Russian strategy probably includes other methodologies to negatively impact Biden's job ratings which would improve Trump's chances for re-election. The majority of the U.S. voting public does not grasp the extent of Russian influences in their daily lives or how those influences impact the political choices they make.

<u>Two-Party Political System</u> – The political stalemate in our country's Capitol has prevented our democracy from operating. The flag of hatred has infiltrated our two-party political system. Gone are the days when members of Congress could have different political affiliations and opinions but still work toward the common good. In reality, it doesn't matter who we send to Washington, D.C. as our representatives because the federal government has become perverted in so many ways – and more so when Trump was in the White House. The damage Trump did to our government is still lingering after his violent and ugly departure.

More importantly, this party division in our country went from a tradition of "extending a hand across the aisle" previous to 2000, to now in 2023, we are so divided we could be living in two different nations. So what happened in the year 2000 to cause or assist this U.S. internal rift and the government dissention in Washington, D.C. and across our nation?

In 2000, Vladimir Putin became the president of Russia.

This is a man who has spent his entire life as a Russian secret service intelligence officer, a spy, before becoming the President of Russia. He thinks the U.S. should be wiped off the face of the earth, because he blames the U.S. for the breakup of the Soviet Union. Over the last twenty-three years, Putin has consistently worked to create a divide in our country for one reason – a country divided is weaker.

Let's put the pieces of this puzzle together. The blind loyalty of millions of Republican Americans to Donald Trump is the elusive piece of the puzzle that evaded my understanding. How could so many smart Americans believe Trump's lies and fanatical speeches, his constant remarks full of hatred, and his crazy conspiracy stories?

Trump was in Russia many, many times
from 1990 to 2020.

GERMANY   RUSSIA

Hitler practiced brainwashing techniques on German public; entire nation became violent.

Putin learned brainwashing techniques while in Germany for many years as <u>a KGB spy</u>.

Putin perfected bribery techniques using drugs and pornography while in Germany.

Putin "possibly" used pornography for bribery of Trump who is an easy target regarding beautiful women. U.S. banks refuse to loan money to Trump, so he did business with Russians which is very dangerous.

Putin wants USA out of NATO and USA troops out of Germany.

Balance of world military power then tilts in favor of Russia.

PIECES OF THE PUZZLE

USA

Trump's speeches full of hatred and lies repeated over and over, which are brainwashing techniques successfully used in dictatorship countries.

Millions of Americans believe Trump's hateful lies and conspiracy stories. In 2020, violence in the U.S. increases by 30% with 7,700 hate crimes. MORE THAN ANY TIME IN U.S. HISTORY.

Trump negates NATO and threatens to withdraw. He pulls USA troops out of Germany and other locations. NATO allies more cautious about partnering with the USA.

Isolationism – USA is a weaker nation.

What is happening in the United States is the same sequence of events that happened in Germany before World War II. Hitler hypnotized an entire nation and converted them from a peaceful population into a violent, hateful, and destructive civilization. He did this through hate propaganda and speeches aimed toward Jews, repeated over and over, until every person in Germany believed his trickery and lies. The result was mass murder, destruction, torture, and a country filled with mindless puppets performing Hitler's insane instructions – until the rest of the worlds' governments/military and a world war stopped his madness. Fear was Hitler's essential tool, but so was manipulative "mob mentality" and persuasion. <u>Trump has used all these mind altering techniques during his four years in the White House and afterwards</u>. Americans have blindly followed him and listened to him and supported him. This is appalling. Come on folks, we are all smarter than this!

Putin spent the majority of his dedicated KGB years in Germany, and had a connection to the Red Army Faction[9], which was a latent terrorist group. Putin studied the history of Germany and spoke German very well. He was thoroughly informed of the destructive influential methods used by Hitler to transform the minds of millions of people. Other history records show Putin created a plan involving blackmail of a German professor[10] using drugs and pornographic material. Putin's relationship to Germany and their horrific history[11] was the missing link to explain what has been happening from 2016 onward in the United States. The exact same methodologies to alter beliefs and brainwash masses of people were used: Germany (Hitler) –Russia (Putin) –USA (Trump).

As Putin moved up the Russian political ladder and became President, his blind hatred of the U.S. was foremost in his strategic plan. This plan could have included "grooming" Trump. To do this, he possibly used the same ole reliable and perfected Russian spy manipulation tool of acquiring pornographic material which could have been attained when Trump traveled to Moscow. Trump made several trips to Moscow over the last thirty years in his attempt to build a Trump Tower there. However, little did he know that Putin would probably never approve a Trump Tower in Moscow – it would be too ostentatious and western.

After visiting Moscow in 2001, Trump was quoted as saying:[12] "I have just returned from Russia. The women there have no morals. You gotta get out there." What this says is: (1) Trump had no idea of the morals for 99.9% of the women in Russia, and (2) he was referring to Russian prostitutes which work for Putin. As a foreign man in Russia, he was potentially targeted and photographed, and these photos are then used to hold a man – especially a westerner - accountable to Putin. This statement by Trump could be taken as an admission of guilt.

Trump – who's self-focused, egotistical personality is perfect for this role – has copied Hitler's corrosive actions. This has resulted in millions of U.S. citizens believing Trump's lies or literally anything fed to them no matter how preposterous and outlandish it sounded. Most people in the U.S. had no idea that they were being brainwashed. In return, Trump got the attention and devotion of millions of people which he craves, and Putin potentially cultivated an "inside" top-level puppet to destroy the United States.

Faces of the people who attacked the U.S. Capitol looked brain-washed and dazed. TV interviews with elected Republican Senators often are not even logical, including Mitch McConnell. Intelligent American citizens have been persuaded to believe and repeat bizarre lies, which have multiplied via social media, and were served up to them by our past President.

This is all supposition – an educated and experienced guess. This hypothesis was concluded because I understand Putin's history and how he thinks and acts (the Russian side of my brain) and have been a witness to the strange transformation of indoctrinated American minds in our society (the American side of my brain).

Putin's childhood[13] was spent in a tiny, run-down, single-room apartment, with no hot water or even a bathtub.[14] His father suffered injuries in World War II, in Russia it is called the Great Patriotic War, and his mother did odd jobs to support the family. His grades were poor except he excelled in history and in German language courses. Overall he was considered a rebel by Russian standards, yet from a young age his dream was to become a KGB agent. To accomplish his goal, he first needed to obtain a law degree which he accomplished. His time in

Germany fine-tuned his spying skills and eventually he was considered a "Russian James Bond," a title still used today.

The KGB was thought by many to be the largest security service in the world, with more than 480,000 agents.[15] It was suspected to have infiltrated all western intelligence agencies. Today it is known as the FSB or Federal Security Service. In comparison, the CIA is estimated to have about 22,000[16] employees.

In the late 1990s and prior to Putin's presidency, a book surfaced called the *Foundations of Geopolitics,* written by Aleksandr Dugin, but with assistance from General Nikolai Klokotov/General Staff Academy and General Leonid Ivashov/Head of the International Department of the Russian Ministry of Defense. (Putin was suspected to be the ghost writer). This book, which is more than 600 pages, is used by the Russian military for training, for discussions regarding the post-communist era, and for outlining plans for achieving Russian inter-national dominance. Included is information on how to (1) infiltrate Western institutions and governments (namely the U.S.), (2) over-throwing Ukraine, (3) endorsing Brexit, and (4) helping France and Germany become strong partners and world powers. Russian government goals outlined in this document cannot be ignored, since indisputably most of these have been realized and/or are currently undertaken by Putin – the master analytic and strategic chess player.

Americans need to comprehend the magnitude of this threat. Putin has targeted the United States any way possible - especially by cyber-attacks on our vital government infrastructure computer systems and our goods and supplies delivery chains. This includes manipulating Trump.

TIME TO WAKE UP AMERICA!

Let the factual documents and proven evidence speak for themselves.   .

"Don Putin," Artist – Hajo de Reijger, Courtesy of Cagle Cartoons

Putin was inaugurated as President of Russia on May 7, 2000[17] Previously, he was serving as a KGB/FSB officer working in East Germany then as a government official in St. Petersburg, Russia. He was picked by Boris Yeltsin to be Prime Minister. Yeltsin succumbed to alcoholism and resigned, upon which Putin became Acting President and later elected as President.

I lived in Moscow during this period and quickly learned how ruthless Putin could be. An example was when a group of forty Chechen militants captured and took control of the Dubrovka Theater in Moscow, demanding that Putin withdraw Russian troops from Chechnya.[18] They took more than 800 hostages, most of them children. The standoff lasted only three days before the Chechnya rebels killed two Russian women. In response, Russian forces piped toxic gas (a poison) into the theater, killing forty-one attackers and 129 young Russian hostages.[19] Putin ordered the attack that poisoned those Russian children, which in turn consolidated his grip on power. Meanwhile, Vladimir Pronichev, who managed this horrific operation, was awarded by Putin the title of "Hero of the Russian Federation."

The first day of school in Russia is something of a holiday, as students arrive in their best clothes bearing flowers for their teachers. Girls normally wear a large bow in their hair.[20]

"But on Sept. first, 2004, armed Islamist extremists seized School Number One in Beslan, in the North Ossetia region of Russia. They demanded Russia remove forces from Chechnya and recognize the separatist region's independence. Radical Chechen warlord Shamil Basayev ordered the attack, but Chechen rebel leader Aslan Maskhadov denounced the move. The extremists held more than 1,100 hostages over three days until Russian forces stormed the building. More than 300 people were killed. Only one hostage-taker, Nur-Pashi Kulayev, was captured alive. He was sentenced to life in prison in 2006."[21]

Putin and his government were criticized for refusing to negotiate and for triggering explosions that killed many, including 186 Russian children. To further explain, children in Russia are highly valued and safeguarded. Most Russian families only have one child, and therefore there is an overwhelming sense of appreciation and protection toward each child. Usually a grandmother (Babushka) cares for the child during the day while parents work. When I told Russian friends that I had four children, they would comment that I am a hero. Understanding this cultural attitude and way of life, I felt comfortable bringing my children to Russia – a mistake that I readily acknowledge.

The European Court of Human Rights ruled that Russia failed in its handling of the crisis that killed 186 children. [22]. Illarionov, Putin's economic adviser at the time, said he couldn't deal with the consequences and the number of children killed. He moved to the U.S. and assumed the job as a senior researcher at The Cato Institute, a libertarian think tank in Washington, D.C." [23]   In 2022, Illarionov was interviewed on "Newsnation" and the commentator said, "There may not be anyone in America who understands the workings of the Russian economy like you do. When you see sanctions now that are put on Russia oligarchs (due to the Ukrainian War), do you think that they're significant enough to have an impact that might sway oligarchs and that might move powerful people against Vladimir Putin?[24]

One of the greatest misconceptions in the West and the United States is the role of the so-called Oligarchs in the Russian economy and the Russian political system. These roles are next to zero. I've heard so much through all these years about the oligarchs, about how it is important to put sanctions on or how to put them in a very different position. If you'd like to make life miserable for those people, it's OK. But if you think those sanctions would make changes in the decision-making process of Mr. Putin or the Kremlin, it's wrong. It's a mistake.

The political system and political regime in Russia is not like the United States or in any Western countries. It is NOT a democracy. It is not even a semi-democracy. It is even not an authoritarian regime anymore. Right now, it's a totalitarian regime and is just a one-man show … You can punish 145 million Russian citizens and it will not change the decision-making process of Putin … It has been Putin's dream for decades to destroy Ukraine.

If Putin is not stopped, he would continue on. It will mean thousands or tens of thousands more will die. He is already responsible for many deaths … calculated it may be up to 500,000 or 600,000 deaths in Russia and outside Russia. How long should we (the U.S. and the world) tolerate this endless spiral of deaths produced by one person?

His goal is not only to stop in Ukraine, his goal is to move into Europe. His goal is to return NATO to the 1997 division line, which means the so-called de-NATO-ization of all countries in Central and Eastern Europe, including Baltic countries, Poland, Romania, and Bulgaria. Putin must be stopped NOW and not allowed to destroy other countries and obliterate more lives. Ukraine is his testing ground, and so far the West has not done enough to prevent his daily onslaught and bombing of hospitals, schools, apartment buildings and other civilian properties. The West may not want to be at war with Russia, but they also may have NO CHOICE.[25]

"Boris Nemtsov, Russian opposition leader and once a contender for the presidency, was shot and killed near the Kremlin on February 27, 2015. Russian authorities investigated Chechen rebels as suspects in the murder, but the politician's daughter, Zhanna Nemtsova, accused Putin of being politically responsible. Nemtsov had been a powerful political opponent of Putin's and worked to expose Russia's secret military campaign in eastern Ukraine."[26] The majority of Russians who would discuss this killing accused Putin of the murder. It is the author's opinion that most Russians are correct.

U.S. authorities suspect Russian interference in the U.S. 2016 presidential elections, prompting a long investigation by U.S. Special Counsel Robert Mueller. In 2018, a Russian internet agency and more than a dozen Russians were charged with interfering in the US election campaign from 2014 through 2016 in a multipronged effort to support then-businessman Donald Trump and disparaging his rival Hillary Clinton. Russia denied interfering in the election and Trump denied any collusion by his campaign. However, the Mueller report, released in April 2019, shows "evidence of numerous links" between officials working on Trump's presidential campaign and individuals "having or claiming ties to the Russian government."[27]Russia later admitted openly to their involvement.

Of course Trump has ties to Russia. If the U.S. Government and the U.S. populace better understood how Russia operates, they would unanimously grasp the concept that Trump and NBC could not have held the Miss Universe contest in Moscow in 2013 without solid ties to "someone" holding immense power in Russia. This event would not have been allowed or approved otherwise. I am sure that Putin received his share of the proceeds.

The connections between Russia and the U.S. are boundless, as are the ties between Trump and Putin. Trump has longed for a Trump Tower in Moscow, and the only signature required to solidify this transaction would be Putin's or someone working for Putin. Trump, on the other hand, has no idea of the "real world" concerning business as a foreigner in Moscow or anywhere in Russia. Perhaps he should call Chuck Norris, who half-owned the Beverly Hills nightclub, restaurant, and casino in Moscow and who lost every dollar invested. His Russian partner, Mayor Lyushkov of Moscow simply no longer wished to have a western partner or half-ownership. He wanted to be the sole owner.

As previously mentioned, my daughter Lize managed the Chuck Norris Moscow business. She died in 2016 and the Tokyo police ruled her death a homicide. Was her death due to the long arm and patience of Russian vengeance? I will never know for sure, but because I lived in Russia for a long, long time, because I became "Russianized," and because I understand that nation and society as well as I understand the U.S., I know that her death will forever remain a painful mystery.

Trump's dictatorship traits mirror Putin's governing style. Trump sued just about everyone who opposed him or bullied them so they lost their employment and reputations. His New York-based organization is under investigation for multiple tax law violations and as of March 2023 Trump has been indicted on thirty criminal charges in New York. No District Attorney in the United States would bring charges against a former President, unless their investigation had found solid evidence to prove their case.

Americans are incredibly naïve. Since the Trump indictment, Trump has raised over $5 million dollars (in 48 hours) by Trump sympathizers.[28] He loves to play the "victim" and Americans "buy" into his barefaced lies that he was indicted due to political persecution and vindication.[29]

American taxpayers were required to pay our taxes, while a man who was our President used his position for personal gain and avoided paying taxes. Trump set a lethal example by politicizing the wearing of masks. As of September 2021 over 42 million Americans have tested positive to Covid-19, some had lung transplants, and by 2022 over one million Americans died due to Covid-19.

Stalin did much the same thing by preventing the shipment of food to specific regions of the USSR. More than twenty million Russians starved to death under Stalin. Putin has gassed, shot, imprisoned, bombed, and poisoned his opponents including thousands of innocent children. Hitler murdered over 6,000,000 Jews. None of these men lost sleep over the deaths of hundreds of thousands of human beings. Trump tear-gassed innocent and legal demonstrators in the street in Washington, D.C. so he could walk across the street, stand in front of a church he does not attend and hold up a Bible. The reason for this action was that many of his "followers" live in the Bible-belt regions of the U.S. These uninformed and blind individuals have contributed millions upon millions of dollars to support Donald Trump in his effort to oppose our democracy and our land of law and order. For Trump, this is nothing more than another scam and money in his pocket. The persons being scammed are those shelling out money for Trump's political campaign.

Title: "Trump Crosses Lafayette Square," Artist – R.J. Matson, Courtesy of Cagle Cartoons.

Most Americans do not realize that Trump has followed the Putin "playbook" to a tee! I watched local Russian TV in Moscow as Putin took office as the President of the Russian Federation the first time. I also read the local and international news and listened to Russian citizens talk about the deaths of various reporters (those who opposed him), the corporate take-overs as leaders of major corporations were falsely accused, subjected to sham trials, and were then sent to prison – all so Putin could personally grab their corporations and assets. Still more of his opposition was deliberately poisoned or shot. Poison is a common lethal method used in Russia to eliminate opposition.

"Putin's Denial," Artist – Jeff Koterba, Courtesy of Cagle Cartoons.

Trump's tactics were frighteningly similar to Putin's – constant disparaging remarks about reporters, firing a long list of staff members, suing anyone who contested him, and ruining the lives of career U.S. Ambassadors, senior military personnel, personal attorneys, and others. Anyone who opposes Trump could be the next name on his hit list. Under Trump's grotesque leadership, our freedom of speech, one of the backbones of our democracy, was butchered.

There are numerous reports of Trump and his followers threatening people's lives and their children. He has incited violence where five Americans lost their lives – most of them while protecting the U.S. Capital. After his indictment in March 2023, "Trump ramped up the attacks on the probe and the district attorney, warning of 'potential death and destruction' if he was charged."[30] Why would anyone want to vote for this man to lead a democracy? Trump appears to be as violent as Vladimir Putin.

While most American politicians and others boast that we "won" the cold war, this war never ended in the mind of President Putin and other Russian government officials. He has and will continue to do anything possible to destroy the U.S. And while this Russian destruction is constant and obvious, Americans just go about their daily lives and are blind and ignorant to the reality of Russian daily assaults on our democracy. This compliancy may not be reversed, and we may lose our freedoms and our form of self-government just because we lethargically sat by and let it happen.

> **This planned devastation of the US possibly included helping Trump gain control of the White House and our democracy in 2016. Trump then became Putin's wrecking ball!**

On Sunday, August 2, 2020, the *New York Times* published an article entitled *John Lewis Was the Anti-Trump*.[31] The following is a quote from this article.

In his final essay, published on Thursday in the New York Times, Representative John Lewis of Georgia offered welcome words of encouragement and wisdom for everyone protesting discrimination and injustice. He also made a crucial point about our political system, one that bears repeating as we face powerful threats to self-government and the rule of law. "Democracy is not a state," Lewis wrote. "It is an act and each generation must do its part to help build what we called the Beloved Community, a nation and a world society at peace with itself."

Representative Lewis dedicated his life to saving our democracy and way of life. He believed in the ideals embodied in the U.S. Constitution that say "justice for all" and "freedom of speech." In the U.S., the practical virtues of representative democracy as a form of governance are tethered to a see-saw. It is up to each of us to ensure that our country and our democracy survive. If you wish to live in a democracy that ensures justice for all and you value your freedom of choice, speech, and opinions, then it's time to stand up and be counted.

Every citizen of this country – Republicans, Democrats, Independents, and everyone else MUST stand up to the injustices across the USA. It is our responsibility and duty. Our country is under attack and we must all work together to prevent the downfall of our democracy. It is time to separate the lies from the truth and reward right while denouncing wrong.

Listen to some of the words sung by Joe South in "Games People Play" which refer to life in the United States.

Oh the games people play now, Every night and every day now, Never meaning what they say now. . .God grant me the serenity, To just remember who I am, 'Cause you've given up your sanity, For your pride and your vanity, and Turn your back on humanity. . .[32]

It is our responsibility and duty as a citizen to deal with this reality and NOT believe the lies fed to us by Trump and by FOX news who have admittedly said they fed the American public fake news about Trump's lie of the election being stolen. Half of the U.S. listened to FOX News and believed their counterfeit and forged messages. WAKE UP AMERICANS AND START TO PUT THE PIECES OF THE PUZZLE TOGETHER.

> **This hatred must stop because it is being used as a weapon to destroy our country.**

We must not let another Black or Hispanic man or woman be murdered due to racism and blind hatred. We must not repeat the horrific history of Nazi Germany, where people followed and blindly worshiped one man who led them into a world war that killed millions of innocent people in concentration camps and on battlefields.

Trump, with his similarities to Putin, his belief in White supremacy, his comments that the KKK are "fine people" (see page 8), and his sending federal troops to intimidate peaceful demonstrators are all serious indications that should not be ignored. Russian hacking of U.S. Government infrastructure systems is also a serious sign. The Cold War of the 2020's looks very different than the Cold War of the 50's thru the 80's, but it is still the Cold War – and the U.S. is not winning.

We must strengthen our democracy; advocate for human rights; eliminate our country's debt, reduce our negative trade balance and our dependency on China, and push for a more sustainable future by working together and not against each other. Our government and American technology must catch up to Russia's cyber-attack capabilities, and denounce their aggression.

Change your hatred to compassion, and improve your relationship with your neighbors, especially if they are not the same political persuasion or the color of their skin is different than yours. Learn to appreciate diversity and understand how it contributes to a better world instead of seeing diversity as a threat. You are not a better human being than other races – you are equal.

From 2016 to 2020, our country has been under assault – by two men (Trump and Putin). Those who blindly supported Trump because he is a Republican have only bought into his hatred of others, his daily lies, his unreal and ridiculous conspiracy theories, and helped him destroy our democracy – which is what Putin intended.

Trump did not win the 2020 election folks; he lost – but not until he developed a cult of violent followers who attacked our Capitol building. They were shouting "where is Nancy, Pence is a traitor, and hang Mike Pence." They even constructed gallows to kill Vice President Pence! If they had found him, he could have been murdered. He was protected by the Capitol Police. Some of those police officers died on January sixth doing their duty to protect the Capitol, to shield and to guard our elected governmental officials, and to defend our democracy.

We need everyone - the men and women of America - to be as brave as these Capitol Police and stand up to defend our democracy. We are all Americans and we have only one country.

Trump did just about everything possible to push his lie that the election was "stolen." In fact, he was just repeating what he said in 2016 after the election when he falsely claimed that Clinton and the Democrats had stolen all the popular votes from him. The exact same "election lie." What does this tell you?

Trump's desperation to retain the presidency, went far beyond a normal desire for power and control. In November 2020 he began (1) filing more than 60 law suits - he lost every single one, (2) scheming for states to create fake electors, and (3) asking various states to overturn legal votes and do re-counts. By December 2020 he was: (4) plotting for Congress to overturn votes, (5) pressuring Pence to stop the election certification, (6) attempting to fire the Acting Director of DOJ and replace him with a man who had agreed to help Trump reverse the election, and was (7) exploring the idea of using the U.S. military under his command to seize voting machines. By January 2021, Trump had (8) instigated a violent attack on the U.S. Capitol building, inspired this mob to hurt or murder Vice President Pence (gallows were created on the steps of the Capitol building and rioters were shouting "hang Mike Pence"), and disrupted the Congressional certification of the 2020 presidential election process that would establish Joe Biden as the next President of the United States. In addition:

"Donald Trump threatened Fox News and it wasn't with a good time. Trump announced on his reportedly financially challenged Truth Social platform that he is considering suing the news network for false advertising after an insulting ad created by The Lincoln Project... The ad is titled 'Sucker," and it basically explains to MAGA Republicans why they are suckers for believing basically anything Trump tells them: Dear MAGA, we have some bad news. No, not that he lost. Not that your little coup attempt failed and its planners and the attackers are going to jail. NO. The really bad news is why Trump told you he lost. Why he set it up way before the 2020 election. It wasn't voter fraud, but it was fraud. Trump told you the election was stolen ripped you off – to sucker you – to take your hard-earned money and shovel it into his pockets.. It was the biggest scam in political history. . . Every dollar you sent him paid to keep his shady business empire and lavish lifestyle going. It was a sucker game all along. And you know who the sucker is? YOU.[33]

These steps engaged over a period of several months validates Trump's despondency, anguish, and DESPERATION to continue as the President of the United

States. The question every American must ask themselves is WHY? Yes, Trump was a sore loser, however his drastic and outrageous behavior was not ordinary (no President in the history of the U.S. has behaved so violently when he lost an election) - UNLESS Trump or a "member of his family" had been threatened by Putin or by someone in the Russian government. This is how Putin operates – he is a mob boss with global outreach. If Putin is pissed – there is no place on this earth to hide from his wrath.

It was only a few months later that Ivana Trump died from a blunt blow to her head. News and media outlets reported that she fell down her apartment steps – the same steps which she successfully navigated daily for decades, and of course it is possible that she did accidently fall. However, her death also could have been a warning to Trump that Putin is not happy with the way things are going in the U.S. and Trump had fallen from grace. If Ivana's death does not put the fear of God into Trump, then he is dimmer than even I believed.

In August 2022, "the mysterious death of a prominent critic of Vladimir Putin's invasion of Ukraine – in a Washington, D.C.'s West-End neighborhood is drawing fury from some of the Kremlin's best-known global detractors – but scant notice in Washington, where police say they don't suspect foul play – it is about Dan Rapoport's fall from a luxury apartment building on the night of August 4th, 2022.[34] Rapoport made a fortune in Moscow and then moved back to the U.S. after running afoul of the Russian Government.[35] In the eyes of Rapoport's political allies, the history of untimely deaths of Kremlin critics makes the (U.S.) police's initial no-foul play conclusion seem naïve."[36] Rapoport was also an open supporter of the jailed opposition leader Alexei Navalny – which Putin loathes. So I seriously doubt that Rapoport – a healthy, middle-aged wealthy man – would throw himself off a balcony on the fifteenth floor of his luxury apartment building. The question is why has the Washington, D.C. police not investigated this death as a murder? Was someone on the police force threatened?

While trusting and ingenuous Americans play their video games and get their "highs" from simulated violence, working with Russians is the real world and it is treacherous. It is time to pull the plug on the video games, and WAKE UP AMERICA. Our country is under attack by a masterful spy, and he sees himself as eventually destroying the U.S. and other European countries.

In *Russian Roulette*, Isikoff and Corn (page. 44) state: "*The Russian intelligence services had become increasingly aggressive and sophisticated in their cyber-attacks, penetrating government, business, and media networks all over the world. Russian hackers showed their might in 2007 when they blitzed Estonia. After the Estonia government removed a statue of a Soviet soldier, a massive cyber-attack shut down the country's banking system, the sanitation system, and the websites of government agencies and news organizations. The country was paralyzed for days. And in 2008, Russian cyber warriors broke into the computers of the U.S. Central Command – which oversaw U.S. military actions throughout the Middle East. . . Other countries have been targeted such as Germany, Poland, the U.K., and France. There was a relationship between France's right-wing National Front led by Marine Le Pen. She had received a $9.8 million dollar loan from a Russian bank. . .*"

When the Russians (Putin) loans money to a politician, the sole purpose is to gain control of that individual. And while Russia loaned Marie Le Pen almost $10 million dollars, the Russians have given Trump far more dollars for real estate deals in the United States.

Putin sees himself as Peter the Great, who lived from 1682 to 1725 and created Russian nobility. Peter the Great is credited with upgrading Russia into the modern age of the 17th century. The frightening part is that Peter the Great also tortured and killed his own son. The radical difference is that Vladimir Putin lives now, and he is reversing his country's progress by centuries instead of modernizing it.

"January Sixth", Artist – David Fitzsimmons, Courtesy of Cagle Cartoons.

> **These assaults on our government and our lives were instigated by Trump but fueled by Putin.**

Now certain individuals in the U.S. Senate are trying to deny that the attack on the Capitol even happened. You and I and everyone else in the U.S. and around the world watched this violent attack on the U.S. Capitol. We watched the destruction of the Capitol building, and of documents, furniture, and other valuable items and artifacts once these people were inside. We saw hundreds of violent people all wearing Trump hats or tee shirts shouting "Save America" while they were attacking the Capitol and the Capitol Police. We all know what happened because it was replayed on television endless times for weeks and months afterward.

What kind of people can deny what they saw with their own eyes? How can a person's mind just plain negate reality? Even former Vice President Pence is now down-playing the January 6th attack. He is lucky he is still alive and apparently this threat did not sink into his brain!

America has been a ripe breeding ground for hatred. Individuals who are easily brain-washed by listening to lies over and over, are also, similar to those individuals who denied the truth about slavery and who hid the Tulsa, Oklahoma massacre – all the while other countries around the globe knew of the massacre and wrote about it in history books. These same individuals spit out discrimination, hatred, racism, and more lies every day in the name of "Save America" – yet go to church on Sunday and swear to love their family and their neighbors. This hypocrisy must stop.

I live in a small mountainous town in a Southwestern state. Our demographics show we have over 16,000 residents and 75% of the population or more are Republicans. This small town has at least thirty churches. There are pockets of men here who collectively think that white supremacy and the neo-Nazi perspective are acceptable. They preach hatred, racism, and believe that Trump was the best President ever to hold the office in the United States. Every Thursday night this local Nazi group meet in a building on Main Street. This is the reality of rural America, and it's frightening.

This is not a game folks, WAKE UP NOW! If we do not protect our democracy and our way of life, tomorrow will be too late.

You will wake up, but you will be living in a country afraid of your local community's police (if you are not already), afraid of what you say and to whom, and you will end up talking to the walls in your home - like I did in Kiev, Ukraine in the early 1990's – because that is where your government will hide their listening devices and their cameras.

Your freedoms will be gone! Our democracy will have died.

At the end of Catherine Belton's book called *Putin's People*, she concludes:

The Russian black-cash networks seemed to be digging in ever deeper. Their activities, combined with Trump's disregard for the institutions and codes of the U.S. democracy, were leading to a systematic standoff. When Trump was caught on a July 27, 2019 telephone call asking Ukraine's new president, Volodomyr Zelenskiy, to meet with Giuliani and press ahead with an investigation into Biden, to many his actions represented an abuse of office. Trump was directly requesting a foreign power to assist him in the 2020 election. Trump appeared to suggest that U.S. military assistance for Ukraine could be contingent on compliance with his request.... This 'irregular policy channel was running contrary to the goals of longstanding U.S. foreign policy.' The only way to deal with it was through an impeachment probe.

The Russians appeared delighted with the chaos, yet also fearful about where impeachment might lead. This scandal exposed both the fragility of the American political system and how it had been corroded....

From the beginning the Russian black-cash networks had, in part, been embedded to erode the (American) system, and exacerbate corruption in the West.... In the impeachment probe and the 2020 U.S. presidential race, the clash between liberal (democratic) values and a Putin-style corrupt authoritarian order was reaching a denouement. 'Putin understands that Russia can spend any amount of money it wants (on sowing chaos in the West).' (Page 488, Putin's People).

Pragmatically, Putin won this round with democracy. The U.S. Senate – replicating the Russian DUMA - had been Trump's ace in a hole and prevented impeachment. It is safe to say that Putin knew this in advance.

This (Russian) network and system of KGB capitalism has infiltrated the West – and is still working twenty-four hours a day. It has penetrated our banks and financial institutions, our consumer supplies, our government vital automated in-

formation systems, our gas, oil, and energy sources, and probably every single aspect of American life.

Putin is not the least bit afraid of the United States, because he probably believes that he is in charge - and our citizens and our elected officials are too naïve to grasp the reality of what this truly means. And according to Catherine Belton, *"All of this was on top of the untold amounts of black-cash being siphoned out of Russia (and into the West) to spend on covert operations to buy foreign (especially American) politicians . . . ."*[37]

And in Russia, President Putin will be sitting in the Kremlin, drinking his Beluga Noble Gold Vodka, and laughing. (Note: Putin actually doesn't like drinking alcohol)[38]

"Putin as Stalin," Artist – Dave Granlund, Courtesy of Cagle Cartoons.

CHAPTER 8 – END NOTES

1 https://www.nontube.cvom. Joe South sang "Games People Play" in 1969.

2 https://en.wikipedia.org_wiki_The_Russia_House. The Russia House is a 1990's American spy film directed by Fred Schepisi and with Sean Connery, Michelle Pfeiffer, Ron Scheider, James Fox, John Mahoney, and others.

3 Ibid.

4 Ibid.

5 https://www.cnbc.com. "The U.S. economy suffered its worst period ever in the second quarter (2020), with the GDP falling a historic 32.9%."

6 ProPublica, January 14, 2021, written by Allan Sloan and Cezary Podkul.

7 https://wwwthebalancemoney.com

8 https://www.apnews.com. "Microsoft: Russia behind 58% of detected state-backed hacks." Written by Frank Bajak, October 7, 2020.

9 Politico.com, June 2020."Did Vladimir Putin support anti-Western terrorists as a young KGB officer?" Written by Catherine Belton, June 20, 2020.

10 https://correctiv.org. "Putin's early years. Putin plans the blackmail of a professor with pornographic material, he employs a notorious neo-Nazi as one of his informants . . ." June 30, 2015.

11 Ibid

12 *Russian Roulette*, Written by Isikoff and Corn, Page 84

13 https://www.pbs.org. "Vladimir Putin's Early Life, Frontline, PBS."

14 Ibid

15 https://www.britannica.com. "Researchers with access to Communist Party archives put the number of KGB personnel at more than 380,000."

16 https://en.wikipedia.org_wiki_Central_Intelligence_Agency.

17 https://en.wikipoedia.org. "First Inauguration of Vladimir Putin."

18 www/history.com

19 Ibid.

20 Ibid.

21 https://www.bbc.com/news/world-europe-3956815. "Beslan school siege: Russia 'failed' in 2004 massacre."

22 Ibid.

23 https://www.prio.org. "What is Wrong with Andrei Illarionov?" Also found on the BBC, April 13, 2017.

24 https://en.wikipedia.org_wiki?Andrey_Illarionov, Interview on Newsnation onMarch 31, 2022.

25 Ibid.

26 https://www.newsweek.com "Zhanna Nemtsova: Why We May Never Know Who Killed My Father Boris." November 11, 2016.

27 https://www.justice.gov-sco-fle. "Report on the Investigation into Russian Interference in the 2016 Presidential Election," Special Counsel Robert S. Mueller, III, March 2019.

28 Axios AM, Written by Mike Allen. Scoop: "Trump raies over $5 million since indictment news."

29 Ibid.

30 Yahoo/news, "Here are the key players in the Trump hush money case," written by Dylan Stableford, March 31, 2023.

31 https://www.nytimes.com. "John Lewis Was the Anti-Trump," July 31, 2020.

32 Joe South, "Games People Play," YouTube, February 8, 2013.

33 Ibid.

34 Politico Magazine, "A Putin Critic Fell from a Building in Washington, D.C. Was it Really a Suicide?", Written by Michael Schaffer, August 26, 2022.

35 Ibid.

36 Ibid.

37 Catherine Belton, Putin's People, Page 493.

38 https://putinhere.com. Why does Vladimir Putin prefer vodka to beer? As a number of Russian media wrote, "Vladimir Putin almost never drinks, especially in public."

Chapter Nine

Final Notes From The Author

I do not undertake this writing and this investigation of racism, hatred and violence in the U.S. as an unbiased bystander. I grew up during the Martin Luther King Jr. days with parents who were both racists. I saw the ugliness from an observation seat at the dinner table. I argued nightly with my father about the lack of logic and compassion for others he was spitting out in such a hostile tone. I asked him to prove what he was saying, but he could not.

Yet my father also regularly told me that "I am no better or worse than anyone else." Instead of buying into his racist remarks, my love for my father allowed me to overlook his inhumanity.

My first husband was a Conservative Jewish boy from New York with a brilliant mind. His father was a Cantor, and both his parents had survived the Holocaust as children. My new name was very "Jewish-New York" sounding, and I remember going to a dry cleaner in San Diego where the owner/operator was from the Mid-East. He asked if I was Jewish, and I unsuspectingly said, "Yes." He refused to take my clothes. I was in my mid-twenties and this was my first experience with any form of "hatred and racism" toward me in the U.S. My first husband died too young of a brain tumor, but he passed along his brilliance to two beautiful daughters.

By my mid-thirties, I worked at Science Applications International Corporation (SAIC) as the Data Base Manager for the largest Russian-language military, technical, and intelligence library in the U.S. We played the "red" team on the White House War Games. SAIC trained me to read, write, and speak Russian. While employed by them, I began traveling to the Soviet Union and, over time, became one of the few Americans living and working in Russia for decades. I became bicultural and multilingual.

My younger two children from my second marriage attended Moscow Public Schools and also learned to speak Russian. My second oldest daughter visited on spring and summer breaks from college and my oldest daughter came to Russia in the early 1990s for a surprise visit for my birthday. She never returned to live in the U.S. Over time, she became fluent in Russian as well as other complex languages such as Japanese, Farsi, Arabic, Danish, and Swahili. She managed several large restaurants in Moscow (one American owner of a restaurant was deliberately killed in a car accident) including the Beverly Hills. She eventually left Russia and became the International Marketing Manager for a large Danish furniture complex. It seemed that Lize was always running to catch an airplane to fly somewhere in the world. She especially loved Abu Dhabi, Tokyo, and Nairobi.

Having lived under the oppressive orthodoxy of Communism, I absorbed and learned numerous chilling "lessons" on Soviet then Russian official egoism, bureaucracy, and absolute rule – a dictatorship. I also learned to love Russians. There is a Russian saying that "Russians are not happy unless they are crying." This depth of emotion and of "Russian souls" is reflected in their amazing culture, art, theaters, and in everyday life. More often than not, Russians ride the subway to work and spend this time reading classic Russian novels or newspapers. They are an educated society, value their edification, and admire intellect in others.

I spent many weekend hours at the Bolshoi Theater in Moscow and the Mariinsky Theater in St. Petersburg. Every December, my children and I witnessed the Nutcracker Ballet danced at the Bolshoi. It is dazzling and resplendent. I have seen the Nutcracker danced in other cities known for their excellent ballet troupes, but none compare to the Bolshoi. The entire theater – exterior and interior - sets the ambiance and excitement.

Many Russians will tell you that Americans have a "soul or spirit" (dysha) that ends in their throat as they are prone to spit out false stories or flat out egotistical lies; a Russian soul reaches to the deep depth of their gut. Their civilization goes back thousands of years, and our history is a short few hundred. However, the United States and Russia are inextricably linked together – which most Americans simply do not grasp. This book is written as a wake-up call. Americans can no longer be naïve about Russia.

In Russia, there is a solid separation between the rulers and the ruled. From Ivan the Terrible to the late 1980s under the Soviets, authoritarian government was embedded into the Russian man and woman on the street. The atrocious and merciless hardships Russians endured over the centuries have generated and shaped a society of people with an unfathomable depth of humanity.

Let me be open and clear, I love Russia - the loving people, the society, the beautiful traditions, the amazing culture, the delightful language, and the human warmth of every Russian on the street. I do not love the Russian government or communism, or the ruthless Russian underworld, or their combative but secretive worldwide aggression. Putin oversees the oligarchs and KGB men and women outside of Russia, and many of them live in the United States or Europe.

I attribute my admiration of Russian society to my many Russian friends and others who I was privileged to meet. Yuri had been the Deputy Director of the USSR Ministry of Finance; and Lidiya had been a history professor at MGU (Moscow State University). Lidiya's husband was a respected and venerated writer. I used to visit his grave at the Novodevichy Cemetery with Lidiya every year on the anniversary of his death. I lived with Lidiya off and on for well over a year before moving to Moscow. In her very small kitchen, her friends and relatives taught me every-day and slang Russian, and how to tell the "good guys from the bad guys (moshennik)." When the hot water was turned off in Moscow every spring and summer months (so the city could clean the centralized pipes) she would boil water for me and help me take a daily bath. The bread factory was across the street from her apartment building. The aroma was breathtaking and I used to buy Russian Black bread for her daily. We would eat the bread with the delicious borshch or shchi soup that Lidiya would prepare and serve with Russian hand-made sour cream (Smetana). When the Soviet Union fell, Lidiya missed the privileges she previously enjoyed as a Communist like access to a western-style grocery store. She loved to buy western butter and coffee there.

Sasha worked for the number one government Russian TV channel until the early 1990s, and later became a manager at Cargill. I would not have survived in Russia without Sasha's help, guidance, and love. When two Russian teen boys took my younger daughters to Gorky Park one evening and abandoned them, Sasha drove from his apartment way out in the southern (Yuzhny) region of Moscow to the Park and rescued them in the middle of the night.

Sergei worked in Foreign Affairs. He was a key confident for endless years and is now a diplomat for Putin's government. We still communicate from time to time.

Zhana Nicholayevna Bydyonia was among those I worked with, but also someone who helped me during the difficult first few years. Zhana, who had a doctorate in Mathematics, was/is the Director of an enormous Russian factory along the Moscow River. This is GOST – the Russian Government Standards Factory that tests and approves every single item manufactured/created within Russia or was transported to Russia. My first office in Russia was in Zhana's building.

When I first moved to Russia, I shipped, via a large cargo ship, 32 packed boxes in a container that also had the first Cadillac to be sent to Russia. In those boxes were winter clothes, boxes of American food like macaroni and cheese, cake mixes, breakfast cereal, and a large artificial Christmas tree. Only 31 boxes made it through Customs. The Christmas tree was stolen. Because Russians do not celebrate Christmas on December 25th, another Christmas tree was hard to find in Moscow. I still wanted my children to celebrate Christmas. Sasha drove me around Moscow until we found a place selling very skinny cut trees for one dollar.

I bought two of them and we tied them together. My son and daughter made ornaments and popcorn. We had a delightful Christmas after all.

The only way my boxes were allowed through Customs without an enormous bribe (about $5,000) was because Zhana called the head of Russian Customs and told him these boxes were to be delivered to her factory.

Due to her family connections, Zhana was a close associate or friend to all the former Soviet Communist leaders and she grew up in the backseat of Russian Zil's (limousines) going eighty miles per hour (roughly 128 kilos) in and out of the Kremlin. She walks with a limp because one of those Zils hit another car when she was five years old.

When Putin took office in 2000, he created a magnificent and sizable mauve velvet-covered book called *Famous Women in Russian History*. As a gift, he gives copies of this book to visiting dignitaries and presidents from around the world. This book cannot be purchased, and a bibliophile told me it is priceless. Zhana Nickolyavna has a full-page description with her photo in the book. She gave me an autographed copy, which is a cherished and treasured memento of my time in Moscow.

As a greeting, the French will kiss someone twice – once on each cheek. In Russia, you will be kissed three times. In the U.S., "personal space" is about 2 feet apart. Russians laugh at the American idea of personal space, because in Russia, people stand nose-to-nose and walk hand-in-hand. It is a delightful way to connect with friends, family, and even acquaintances. Russians will accept and love you – while in the U.S., it can be difficult to make new friends. I truly miss the physical and emotional closeness of the Russian people, and I miss my own Russian soul – a kinder, more-gentle, and loving person – someone who is wiser and more intuitive than the American side of my brain.

To buy groceries, my youngest daughter and I would walk to the store arm and arm like other Russian families. We have not done this since living in Russia and I truly miss this physical closeness.

I learned many life lessons and among them was humility. I came to terms with how little I, as an arrogant American, really knew of other countries, cultures, and people. As an American, I thought that I was better in some way, but quickly learned that simply was not true. Even more, I knew nothing of what the rest of the world – especially Russians – thought of Americans. While learning to live on the streets of Moscow and St. Petersburg, half of my brain was still beating the drum of democracy and self-determination. The reality was that in Russia or any dictator-lead country, I could be incarcerated at any time for any reason. I had no rights. Living daily knowing that you have no legal or civil rights results in a very deep appreciation and understanding of the privilege called "democracy."

While in Moscow, we had an armed break-in at our apartment near the Kazansky Railroad Station. Five masked and armed men tied up our Russian driver, my son, and my daughter. When they attempted to tie me up, I screamed, bit, clawed, and fought as hard as possible. They then grabbed my daughter and put a gun to her head. I stopped resisting. They stole everything of value that we owned except some cash I had hidden. I was pulled around the apartment by my hair and asked where they could find cash. Towards the end of this horrific experience, they turned up the volume of the TV. At this point, I surely thought that they would kill all of us. My daughter asked me to climb on top of her on the floor in an effort to protect her, which I did. They warned us that if we left the apartment within two hours, we would be killed.

Initially, I thought this attack was because I had learned about a massive crooked deal between an American from Florida doing a pharmaceutical contract with former Soviet officials of the USSR and a contract with the U.S. Government. I had informed the U.S. Government of the details of the deal, and they broke off the contract with the man from Florida. This was a multi-million-dollar contract. Two years later I learned the true reason for the break-in.

Afterward, I called the U.S. Embassy and learned that they could do nothing to help. Their only recommendation was that we stay at the Radisson Slavinskaya Hotel for the weekend. The local Russian police laughed at my request to search for those who committed this crime. They would make an effort to solve this crime only if they received a large bribe or if I asked Zhana to call them. Both of my children were immediately booked on flights back to the U.S. and I stayed for three months in Sasha's grandmother's vacant apartment. I bought a gun and learned to use it, but I desperately missed my children. It felt as though someone had pulled my heart right out of my body.

Many Americans came to Russia thinking that as an American, they are entitled to the same freedoms and civil liberties they enjoy at home in the U. S. Some of those individuals have been killed due to their lack of knowledge and/or absence of experience. This was especially true of those who formed joint ventures with Russian partners. Americans generally found it difficult, if not impossible, to transition or understand Russia and Russians. Most Americans worked with translators, but unbeknown to them the translators deliberately did not provide truthful or accurate information most of the time – leaving the American misinformed and easy to manipulate. The American JV partner would contribute expertise and money, and the Russian partner would contribute the legal and local connections. Routinely, the Russian partner would decide when they had absorbed enough "western expertise" or received adequate investment dollars. The westerner would have a car accident, end up in the Moscow River; or several individuals were thrown out of windows in Moscow's tall apartment buildings. If they were lucky, the Russian would simply tear up the joint venture documentation and prevent the western partner from obtaining a new travel Visa in order to re-enter Russia. When I was in Central Asia, one American woman doing a publishing joint venture with an Uzbek educational firm was found butchered, cut up, and shoved into a large wooden trunk in her apartment. Variations of this pattern was consistent throughout the former Soviet Union and was experienced by large gas and oil companies, restaurants, western stores, and even small U.S.-Russian joint ventures.

I was living in Moscow during the 1991 collapse of the Soviet Union and during the 1993 Russian coup. The week before Yeltsin bombed the Russian White House, I had a meeting with the Minister of Information on one of the top floors. I was the sole representative in Russia for Janes Military Books based in London. We became close friends and still communicate. It was my relationship with him that made this historical event very personal for me.

Russian history entered an entirely new era after the bombing of the Russian White House. Prior to this, there was no pornography legally allowed in the USSR. In the new more free period, the impact of a sexual revolution was seen everywhere. Evidence of its impact on Russian families resulted in a soaring number of divorces and abortions, increased numbers of families giving their children to Russian orphanages known as "social orphans," and the purchasing of material goods along with the pervasive impact of "westernism." Even more evident was the breakup of traditional and cherished Russian values. As a misplaced immigrant to Russia, I also missed the old-world Russian traditions.

In the process of absorbing another culture, I became acutely aware of the Russian and Central Asian man-on-the-street view of the United States. On September 10, 2021, Fareed's Global Briefing stated:[1] "The *Economist* writes...Not only has America failed to strengthen an international order that conforms to its values, America's own public institutions and many of its private ones – whether from confusion, exhaustion, fear, or partisan-political assault – are also emerging weaker from this twenty-year experiment in power projection."

What Zakaria and *The Economist* called the U.S. "twenty-year experiment in power projection," I would substitute the word "aggression" for "projection." Almost half the world thinks of the United States as an antagonistic, violent, and confrontational nation – a country that starts wars and destroys homes and lives. The other half of the world thinks of the U.S. as the world's only "shinning knight that saves democracy and freedom."

There should be a discussion regarding the U.S. Military power structure and why some other nations view our country as provocative and combative. As a nation, we should be grateful to General Milley who prevented Trump's anger from erupting into a dangerous war. However, the Pentagon welds enormous influence on U.S. international policies and history demonstrates that the U.S. is prone to implement more offensive strikes than defensive military responses.

According to the New York Times, the Washington Post, and several other news media sources, the U.S. military launched a drone missile attack in Kabul on August 29th, 2021. This was after the U.S. total withdrawal from Afghanistan.

The strike hit an erroneous target and struck a home and a car owned by an Afghan humanitarian aid worker who wanted to leave Afghanistan.[2]

"General McKenzie, head of U.S. Central Command confirmed that a U.S. drone strike in Kabul, Afghanistan on August 29, 2021 killed 10 civilians, including an aid worker and seven children...The Center for Civilians in Conflict expresses deep condolences to the families of those killed, the latest of <u>tens of thousands</u> of likely civilian casualties from U.S. airstrikes over the last two decades... The U.S. Military's prompt investigation, public acknowledgement, and apology, as well as reports that the U.S. military is conducting further investigations into the strike and considering offering condolence payments to the families ..."

The media reported that the American drone killed three adults and seven children, including two three-year-olds. Details of the U.S. military strategy behind this launch were sketchy, but the Pentagon is now calling it a "mistake." This type of unacceptable and inhumane "mistake" is perceived by local residents as American aggression – and offering condolence payments will not replace their loved ones. The lives of these three-year-old children were no less relevant than the life of any three-year-old living in the United States or elsewhere in the world. Similar misplaced U.S. drone strikes have been reported throughout the Mid-East and especially in Afghanistan.

Those American military personnel who launched this attack, while ordered to do so, are the same military personnel who eventually come home after their tour of duty and often become local policemen and women across the U.S. On the home front, their actions are called "police brutality," – yet they are only responding as they have been trained by our military.

In 2000, I was driving from the airport in Almaty, Kazakhstan. There was a poster on a telephone pole that caught my eye. I asked my driver to stop the car and I climbed up the pole – wearing a dress - and retrieved it. Because I cannot get copyright approval to publish a copy of this poster, I can only describe it. The poster was a photograph of an angry President George W. Bush pointing a finger and saying in Russian, "if you do not believe in (our) democracy, we will fly to (attack) your country next." Later I learned that this poster was seen all over Central Asia and was believed to be the work of a local division of al-Qaeda.

This poster of President Bush was found twenty-one years ago. It was only six months later that commercial airlines flew into the Twin Towers in New York, the Pentagon in Washington, D.C., and a field in Pennsylvania – but was intended to hit the nation's symbol of democracy – the Capitol.

Bin-Laden wanted Americans to suffer and to be on the receiving-end of a terror campaign. He succeeded and nearly 3,000 Americans died that day.

I can picture bin Laden sitting on a cloud and shouting down at Trump who is golfing. Osama would say "thanks to Trump for attacking the U.S. Capitol which was the only target he missed on 9-11". Trump would respond, "Your welcome, pal".

Every individual in the United States felt this was an unprovoked attack on American soil and American lives – and therefore, the only resolution was the Afghanistan War on terrorism.

President Bush took every action necessary or possible to protect Americans and to hunt down bin-Laden. However his approach was incorrect. American troops bombed cities in Afghanistan and searched caves across this vast country. Bin Laden was not found in Afghanistan nor was he found in a cave. He was eventually found in a large house in Pakistan - an entirely different country. Only a few years later, former President Bush attacked the country of Iraq searching for "weapons of mass destruction (WMD)". Eventually, it was discovered that there were no WMD's in Iraq but The Military Times reported that the American taxpayers spent $3T dollars on this war. What does this say about U.S. military intelligence?

President Obama and the CIA eventually discovered bid-Laden's location and killed him, but that was in 2011. The war in Afghanistan did not end until 2021 and cost the American taxpayers and our country $2,313 Trillion Dollars.[3] From 2001 to 2021, a total of 243,000 U.S. military and other personnel died in Afghanistan and Pakistan.[4] Was this war worth the cost of lives lost or the dollars spent during the last ten years?

We have a long history of war, and in fact, the United States has been at war every century since we were founded and every decade since the 1930s.[5] This list is not all-inclusive.

- The American Revolutionary War (1775-1783), $1.2 Billion

- The War of 1812 (1812-1815), $7 Million

- The Mexican-American War, (1846-1848), $1.1 Billion

- The American Civil War (1861-1865), $44.4 Billion

- The Spanish-American War (1898), $6.3 Billion

- World War I (1914-1918), $196.5 Billion

- World War II (1939-1945), $2,091 Billion

- Korean War (1950-1953), $263.9 Billion

- The Bay of Pigs Invasion (1961)

- The Vietnam War (1959-1975), $346.8 Billion

- The Persian Gulf War (1990-1991), $61.1 Billion (Preparations began in the late 1980s)

- Intervention in Bosnia and Herzegovina (1995-1996)

- The Iraq War (2003-2011), $1.7 Trillion

- War in Northwest Pakistan (2004 to present), mainly drone attacks.

- Somalia and Northeastern Kenya (2007 to present)

- Intervention in Libya (2011)

- Lord's Resistance Army (2011-2017) U.S. and allies against the Lord's

Resistance Army in Uganda

- U.S.-led Intervention in Syria (2014 to present)

- Yemeni Civil War (2015 to present)

- U.S. Intervention in Libya (2015 to 2020)

- The War in Afghanistan (2001-2021), with a total cost of $2,313T

What have all these years at war taught the American people, including the U.S. Government and our military? Our military, has the largest stockpile of firepower in the world, but also has a distinctive black-mark for being the only country to ever use nuclear weapons in combat. If you sum up the total spent for U.S. wars, what is the cost impact to the U.S. federal budget? If Putin wanted to bankrupt the United States, all he had to do was create another war and "whala" he did just that. As of January 2023, the U.S. has approved $54 Billion dollars[6] on the war in Ukraine to save worldwide democracy.

How many hundreds or thousands of our military men and women have returned to the U.S. after fighting a brutal war, and joined local police forces, and over how many years?

And, yes, Zakaria and *The Economist* was correct; the United States is weaker than we were in 2001. The question is, why? Besides our own governmental bumbling blunders – and there were many, I would provide a different response than most Americans.

Let me repeat - Putin assumed power of Russia in 2000.

From the moment he took the oath of office, he began: (1) a dramatic and quick rise in global power, primarily by accelerating and exploiting oil wealth on a scale that is comparable to Saudi Arabia; (2) fast-tracking growth of Russia's economy at an alarming rate, including paying off Russia's foreign debt and investing in foreign stocks; (3) expanding the KGB/FSB internationally, and (4) persistent and unceasing strategic destruction of his arch-enemy – the United States.

What the West thought was the end of the Cold War in 1991, was only a hiccup in history while Russia rebuilt its resources. Putin, a Cold War-era spy, has continued his vendetta against the USA.

Putin also supported al-Qaeda. It was less than one year later after Putin became the President of Russia, that al-Qaeda attacked the United States on September 11, 2001. Was there a connection?

This poster found in Kazakhstan is not specifically a reflection of President Bush as much as it makes a statement about the anti-American sentiment throughout Central Asia and the Mid-East at that point in time. The 9-11 attacks on U.S. soil were planned for years by the radical Islamic group known as al-Qaeda and headed by Osama bin-Laden. They primarily were located in this region. Regarded as a terrorist group, they were funded by bin-Laden's sprawling and influential family. He received an annual allowance of seven million dollars.[7]

I am deliberately not drawing conclusions but hope that if you are reading this book, you will begin to form your own thoughts about the ties between: President Putin/Russia, al-Qaeda, bin Laden/9-11, U.S. wars abroad, former President Trump, and our own provocation and policies about how the U.S. military operates. Then make the connection between the U.S. military and domestic police brutality, between racism and hatred, and between Trump's many lies, his conspiracy stories, and his dangerous ties to Russia and Saudi Arabia. Ask yourself, did Trump commit treason during his time in the White House?

Former President Trump sold his soul – and our country – to the devil when he did business with or borrowed money from ruthless Russian business men and others from that region. He also might have been compromised using Russian prostitutes. In either case, it appears that his desperate need for more and more money, his lust for women, or his massive ignorance about business with Russians probably resulted in a very typical Russian trap and potential bribery. He, perhaps unknowingly at the time, used our country and our democracy as bait. He was desperate to maintain control of the U.S. not just because he might face new and/or criminal law suits, but because of a more fraught and life-threatening situation. If he was manipulated by Putin – which I believe is what happened - then he or his family was facing life-threatening fears. He therefore created the "big lie", perhaps used Psy-Group[8] to secretly market this disinformation[9], and then instigated an attack on our Capitol in an attempt to overthrow the election – since the presidency was his one and only safety net.

According to the Wall Street Journal, Psy-Group had partnered (before the 2016 election) with Trump to not only distribute "misinformation" but to bid and win business from the U.S. Government once Trump became President in 2016. Trump was looking for another way to profit from his position as the President. Mistakenly, Trump thought that a foreign company could apply for and win (with him in the White House) multi-million dollar U.S. Government contracts and/or grants.

Business men in the entire former Soviet territory operate like spiders catching victims in their webs. Once their prey is ensnared in the trap, there is no escape. Trump was "groomed" years prior to winning the 2016 election, but once he assumed residence at the U.S. White House – he appeared to be under the control of Vladimir Putin, who in turn controls a global network of oligarchs and KGB – ruthless men who are wheeling and dealing in enormous sums of money and unfathomable corruption.

Trump's lack of understanding of Russians extends as well to the Taliban. My friend Sasha was in the Russian-Afghan War. He told me about a horrific incident that still haunts him many years later. He said his military patrol was walking down a street near Kandahar. They came across a young boy who looked about three or four years old. This boy was standing on the side of the road and openly crying. One of the Russian soldiers went over to the boy to ask "what was the matter?" Russian's highly value and protect their children, so this was a natural reaction. When the soldier kneeled down to help, both the boy and the soldier were blown up. This incident was the work of the Taliban.

These fanatical Islamic men are not people to negotiate with or even communicate with. Yet during the Trump Presidency he signed an Agreement with the Taliban – not the Afghan government – to withdraw American troops by May 1, 2021. "Senior military officials in the United States have linked the collapse of the Afghan government and its security forces in August to former President Donald Trump's deal with the Taliban in 2020 promising a complete withdrawal of US troops.[10]

This action would please Putin. Trump never met or spoke with the legal and elected President of Afghanistan – he ONLY spoke with the Taliban. He treated the Afghanistan government -who was supported by U.S. troops and taxpayer money for twenty years - as not important. It is no wonder the Taliban instantly took control of the country; the legal President fled for his life; and all the money invested and American lives lost in this war were no longer as important. It was probably Putin who advised Trump to speak only to the Taliban. WAKE UP AMERICA! He even invited a Taliban leader to join him at Camp David. In August 2021, Mullah Baradar[11], one of the Taliban spokesmen, candidly told the international community and news media that no Afghan should fear for their safety and no one would be harmed after their rapid ascent to power in Afghanistan. One week later, the Taliban beheaded an Afghan police officer[12], and two weeks prior 170 Afghan citizens and thirteen Americans were killed in a car bomb near the airport.[13] As of September 25, 2021, there are now dead bodies[14] hanging in a town square in Kabul. Please remember, this is a group of terrorists that Trump invited to visit him in the United States at Camp David. This invitation demonstrates Trump's vast ignorance and inexperience in dealing with ruthless and coldblooded extremists – and to what extent he will go to please Vladimir Putin.

Eventually, my work led to consulting jobs or employment worldwide: all fifteen former Soviet Republics, Finland and the Netherlands, most of Europe, the Mid-East, the Far-East, Bosnia, India, Pakistan, Afghanistan, Africa, and

South America. My worldwide exposure to different cultures, religions, and people of various appearances, traditions, and governments from democracy to communism to socialism and back – resulted in a more informed perspective on humanity than before I began this global journey.

It's this distinctive view that I bring to this book on racism in America and our country's recent brush with totalitarianism - a dictatorship based on rule by fear.

The very people who should be reading this book probably will not. Judging from the many angry and dazed (almost drugged) faces of those individuals who were present on January sixth while demolishing our nations' Capitol, I doubt they read much of anything outside of a menu at their local drive-up window. However, those very individuals are the targeted audience for the message in this book. Who knows, they may enjoy the cartoons and then grasp the message, the concepts, and the warning intended in this book!

Somehow and someway, the rest of the citizens of the United States need to help these individuals realize that **they and Trump are not and were not saving America but <u>destroying it</u> – through violence, hatred, racism, and ignorance. Brain-washing is reciting and repeating lies, which many news sources have stated is Trumps mode of operation. He even may have employed, directly or indirectly, a company called Psy-Group, who specializes in mass mind manipulation and social marketing, to push his lies and to search for ways to financially benefit from his presidency. Because of Robert Mueller's investigation into Trump and his relationship to Russia, Psy-Group reportedly shut down.**

And the rest of the United States needs to grasp that Russia never ended the Cold War. We let our guard down because we were told that the Cold War era was over. Sorry folks, this is flat out misinformation. You need to understand what this means for yourselves and your families.

United States is still the number one enemy of Vladimir Putin and the Russian Government, and they have used any method possible to destroy our democracy and our freedoms.

This most likely included compromising our President – a man who was easily swayed by the Russians and lured by money and prostitution.

 # WAKE UP AMERICA

Since writing and publishing this book, it appears that the Russians - the long arm of the old KGB and the new FSB - are attempting to locate me via a video phone call with my old friend Sasha.

This book is intended to be a dire WARNING to all Americans. I am now targeted and you could be as well in the near future.

3

EVENTS

Trump "potentially" caught in Russian spy pornography trap. Trump paid hush money to American prostitutes. Putin knew that Trump's weakness is beautiful women.

UNITED STATES

HISTORY LESSONS REPEATED

1985	Putin in Germany as a KGB spy
1991	Iron Curtain fell, Yeltsin was first President of Russia.
2000	Putin becomes second President
2013	Trump visits Russia many, many times.
2014-2015	Trump runs for U.S. Presidency.
2016	Trump becomes U.S. President
2016 – 2020	

U.S. citizens, especially Republicans, subject to hatred/racism, brain-washing, conspiracy theories, and lies. Trump's MO is fear, misinformation, and bullying like a dictator.
2021 Trump-led violent attack on U.S. Capitol.
2020-2021 Trump speaks privately with Putin seven times in 2020 and more in 2021.

Putin maneuvers Trump into the U.S. Presidency and Trump gives Russia what they want: Troop withdraw from Germany and other European countries, U.S. alienation with NATO and western allies. This tilts the worldwide military balance in favor of Russia and isolates the USA.

Trump uses the same type of brainwashing, hatred, and Fear used in Germany before World War II.

Trump's followers attacked the U.S. Capitol on Jan. 6, 2021. U.S. violence increases in 2020, Murders increase by 30%.

HOW PUTIN HOOKED TRUMP

RUSSIA

Putin was a KGB spy in Germany
for many years. He learned Hitler's
techniques and bribery methods
using pornography.

Hitler used hatred
and brain washing to
change the minds of
an entire nation to
enact violence, ethnic
cleansing, and mass
murder.

GERMANY

TIME 100 Edition, June 2022
The Most Influential Persons of 2021-2022

The recent edition of TIME100 Magazine dated June 2, 2022 is dedicated to the most influential persons worldwide. Inside the front cover is the message from the Editor-in-Chief/CEO (Edward Felsenthal) called "Power for Good," where it describes the contents of this edition. (TIME100, page 5) He says "When our team gets together to choose the TIME100, we have one barometer: <u>influence</u>. Who shaped the year? Who stood up? Who stood out? Influence, of course, may be for good or for ill – a dichotomy never more visible than in this year's TIME100, which describes both Vladimir Putin and Volodymyr Zelensky.

This edition includes the Russian dictator (Putin) behind a brutal war, and his foe, the Ukrainian President (Zelensky) whose leadership has made him a rare heroic figure in our divisive time." The description of President Zelensky was written by U.S. President Joe Biden. The description of President Putin was written by Alexei Navalny. For those of you who do not know Navalny, he is the current leader of the Russian opposition, was poisoned by Putin but survived, and is now serving nine years in a Russian maximum-security penal colony. (TIME100, page 65). I am quoting Navalny because I believe that my words could not possibly surpass his in attempting to describe Putin.

Navalny states:

Perhaps Vladimir Putin's true mission is to teach lessons. To everyone – from world leaders and pundits to ordinary people. He has been especially good at this in 2022. He reminded us once again that a path that begins with "just a little election rigging" always ends with a dictatorship.

When I read this statement, all I could think of was President Trump's call (which was taped) to Brad Raffensperger (R), the Secretary of State for Georgia pressuring him to "just find about 11,780 votes" in order to overturn the 2020 presidential election. This was first published by The Washington Post and then The New York Times. Navalny goes on to write:

World leaders have hypocritically talked for years about a "pragmatic approach" and the benefits of international trade. In so doing, they enabled themselves to benefit from Russian oil and gas while Putin's grip on (international) power grew stronger. Between sanctions and military and economic aid, this war (with Ukraine) will cost hundreds of times more than those lucrative oil and gas contracts, the signing of which used to be celebrated with champagne.

Putin has reminded us all of the "duck test": if something looks like a duck, swims like a duck, and quacks like a duck, then it probably is a duck.

The very same logic should be applied in this case: if someone destroys the independent media, organizes political assassinations, and sticks to his imperial delusions, then he is a madman capable of causing a bloodbath in the center of Europe in the 21st century...

However, the answer to the main question he poses – how to stop an evil madman with an army, nuclear weapons, and membership in the U.N. Security Council – is yet to be answered.

And we are the ones who must find that answer.

The Moscow Times, July 12, 2022
"The Unique Banality of Vladimir Putin"

The Russian autocrat is both unique and banal. He is unique in that he established a regime in the 21st century that is more typical of the mid-20th century. In the post-heroic age, which knows no borders for the movement of people, capital and ideas, he staged a theater of the "heroic" defense of a sovereignty that no one had ever attempted to destroy. And he orchestrated the triumph of the practical application of imperialism in an era when no empire exists.

*At the same time, he is as banal as the dictators and autocrats of the 20th century — they are all alike in many ways. They all **fostered the cult of the leader, relied on the indifference and obedience of the masses, deified the state, maintained a cult of strength, militarism and heroic death, confused themselves with the state, built an autarkic economic model, often surviving by extracting rents from resource dependence.** They also **refused on principle to allow a rotation of power,** fought against "national traitors," imprisoned their opponents, imposed censorship, and **sought to rule forever.***

Note From the Author

I subscribe to "The Moscow Times" online. It is the only English-language newspaper in Russia and began publication when I lived in Moscow in the early 1990's. When I read this description of Putin, I wondered if the exact same description could apply to former President Trump?

IT CAN (and is) HAPPENING HERE!!!

FINAL NOTES FROM THE AUTHOR - END NOTES

1 Fareed Zakaria, September 10, 20201 cites an article from The Economist.

2 https://civiliansinconflict.org, September 24, 2021.

3 https://watson.brown.edu. "Human and Budgetary Costs to Date of the U.S. War in Afghanistan since the U.S. invasion in 2001."

4 Ibid.

5 https://en.wikipedia.org_wiki_List-of-Wars-Involving-the-United-States.

6 https://nytimes.com. "Four Ways to Understand the $54 Billion in U.S. Spending on Ukraine." Written by Blanca Pallaro and Alicia Parlapiano, May 20, 2022.

7 https://www.dailytelegraph.com.au. "Osama bin Laden could have spent his life lounging around on his annual allowance of $7 million. Instead, he became the truly global face of terrorism." Written by Janet Fife-Yeomans, May 3, 2011.

8 https://en.wikipedia.org. Psy-Group is a former Israeli private intelligence agency/social media company. It (supposedly) closed after revelations that it was under investigation by Special Counsel Robert Mueller.

9 https://www.wsj.com. "Israeli Intelligence Company Formed Venture With Trump Campaign Firm Cambridge Analytica – who formed a data firm for President Donald Trump's campaign in a joint bid to win business from the U.S. Government and other clients after the 2016 election."

10 https://www.aljazeera.com/news/2021/9/30/us-generals-say-afghanistan-collapse-rooted-in-trump-taliban-deal. 30 Sept. 2021. "U.S. General says Afghanistan collapse rooted in Trump-Taliban Deal."

11 https://crsreports.congress.gov. "Taliban Government in Afghanistan: Background and Issues"

12 https://wwwyoutube.com. "Taliban beheads local Afghan police officer in a chilling video."

13 https://www.nytimes.com. "Lone ISIS Bomber Carried out Kabul Airport Attack, U.S. Says. The suicide bombing killed as many as 170 civilians and 13 U.S. troops in the final days of U.S. military involvement in Afghanistan." Written by Eric Schmitt and Helene Cooper, February 4, 2022.

14 https://nypost.youtube. "Taliban hang bodies of dead 'criminals' in gruesome public display." Written by Kenneth Garger. October 5, 2021.

Bibliography

Anonymous. *A Warning*, "A Senior Trump Administration Official," Twelve, A Hachette Book Group, New York, N.Y., 2019.

Binyon, Michael. *Life in Russia*, Pantheon Books, a division of Random House, Inc. New York, N.Y., 1983.

Belton, Catherine. *Putin's People*, Farrar, Strauss, and Giroux, New York, NY. 2020.

Blackwell, J. Kenneth and Corsi, Jerome R. Ph.D. *Rebuilding America*, "A Prescription for Creating Strong Families, Building the Wealth of Working People, and Ending Welfare," WND Books, Nashville, Tennessee, 2006.

Bloom, Allan. *The Closing of the American Mind*, "How Higher Education has Failed Democracy and Impoverished the Souls of Today's Students," Simon & Schuster, New York, N.Y., 1987.

Bolton, John. *The Room Where it Happened*, Simon & Schuster, New York, N.Y., 2020.

Bottomore, Tom (Editor). *Karl Marx*, Prentice-Hall, Inc., Englewood Cliffs, N.J., 1973.

Bouie, Jamelle, New York Times, Sunday Review Section, August 2, 2020, p. 9.

Cargill, "Statement Regarding Their Russian Operations" www.Cargill.com

CNN, October 7, 2021, Jake Trapper morning show.

Diangelo, Robin. *White Fragility*, Beacon Press, Boston, MA., 018.

Dugin, Aleksandr, *The Foundations of Geopolitics*, Moscow, Russia, 1997.

D'Souza, Dinesh. *The End of Racism*, The Free Press, New York, N.Y., 1995.

Dunn, John. *A History of Democracy*, Atlantic Monthly Press, New York, N.Y., 2005.

Gerzon, Mark. *Global Citizens*, "How our vision of the world is outdated and what we can do about it," Rider, an imprint of Ebury Publishing, a division of Random House Gorup, printed in Great Britian, 2010.

Gorbachev, Mikhail. *Perestroika*, "New Thinking for Our Country and the World," Harper and Row, New York, N.Y., 1987.

Hughley, D.L. and Moe, Doug. *Surrender White People,!* "Our Unconditional Terms for Peace," Harper Collins Publisher, New York, N.Y., 2020.

Isikoff, Michael and Corn, David, *Russian Roulette,* The Inside Story of Putin's War on America and the Election of Donald Trump. Twelve, Hachette Book Group, New York, N.Y. March 2018.

Krugman, Paul. *Arguing with Zombies,* W.W.Norton & Company, New York, N.Y., 2021.

LeVine, Steve. *Putin's Labyrinth*, Random House, New York, N.Y., 2008.

Navalny, Alexei, TIME100 Magazine, June 6-June 13, 2022, page 65, *Vladimir Putin*, a Dangerous Autocrat.

Obama, Barack. *A Promised Land,* Crown, A Registered Trademark of Penguin Random House, LLC., New York, N.Y., 2020.

Politkovskaya, Anna. *Putin's Russia*, A Metropolitan/Owl Book, Henry Hold and Company, New York, N.Y., 2005.

Rashid, Ahmed. *Taliban*, "Militant Islam, Oil and Fundamentalism in Central Asia," Yale University Press, London, England, 2001.

Ringer, Robert J. *How You Can Find Happiness During the Collapse of Western Civilization,* Harper and Row Publishers, New York, N.Y., 1983.

Sandel, Michael J. *Justice*, "What's the Right Thing to Do?" Farrar, Straus and Giroux, New York, N.Y., 2009.

Shalev, Zev, Mundi, Salvator, *The Lost Davinci Story*, January 2, 2019. https://narativ.org/2019/01/02/salvator-mundi-art-of-the-deal-the-lost-davinci/

https://www.dallasnews.com/arts-entertainment/visual-arts/2019/01/27/the-story-of-a-painting-starring-leonardo-da-vinci-trump-russia-a-saudi-crown-prince-and-dallas/

Smith, Hedrick. *The Russians,* Ballantine Books, New York, N.Y., 1977.

Smith, Hedrick. *The New Russians*, Avon Books, New York, N.Y., 1991.

Tayler, Jeffrey. *Siberian Dawn*, "A Journey Across the New Russia," Hungry Mind Press, St. Paul, MN., 1999.

The New York Times, *The January 6 Report*.

Trump, Mary L., PhD. *Too Much and Never Enough*, "How My Family Created the World's Most Dangerous Man," Simon & Schuster, New York, N.Y., 2020.

Williamson, Marianne. <u>Life Magazine</u>, December 1997, page 69.

www.ingramcontent.com/pod-product-compliance
Lightning Source LLC
Chambersburg PA
CBHW062127020426
42335CB00013B/1132